Elements of African Traditional Religion

Elements of African Traditional Religion

A Textbook for Students of Comparative Religion

ELIA SHABANI MLIGO

RESOURCE *Publications* • Eugene, Oregon

ELEMENTS OF AFRICAN TRADITIONAL RELIGION
A Textbook for Students of Comparative Religion

Copyright © 2013 Elia Shabani Mligo. All rights reserved. Except for brief quotations in critical publications or reviews, no part of this book may be reproduced in any manner without prior written permission from the publisher. Write: Permissions, Wipf and Stock Publishers, 199 W. 8th Ave., Suite 3, Eugene, OR 97401.

Resource Publications
An Imprint of Wipf and Stock Publishers
199 W. 8th Ave., Suite 3
Eugene, OR 97401
www.wipfandstock.com

ISBN 13: 978-1-62564-070-3
Manufactured in the U.S.A.

All scripture quotations, unless otherwise indicated, are taken from the Holy Bible, New International Version®, NIV®. Copyright ©1973, 1978, 1984 by Biblica, Inc.™ Used by permission of Zondervan. All rights reserved worldwide.

This book is dedicated to

*Nyumbanitu Traditional Religious Worship Shrine
at Njombe Tanzania,
a well-known Traditional Shrine among the Bena.
I had a high time to Experience and Learn
from the reserved Traditions of my Ancestors*

Contents

Foreword ix
Acknowledgments xiii
Peculiar Features of African Traditional Religion xv

1 Introduction 1

2 Beliefs, Rituals, and Symbols 30

3 The Concept of God 53

4 The Bena Worship at Nyumbanitu Shrine 68

5 African Cosmology 91

6 Concepts of Revelation and Salvation 102

7 Conclusion 110

Bibliography 113

Foreword

IN THIS MAMMOTH WORK, *Elements of African Traditional Religion: A Textbook for Students of Comparative Religion,* Elia Shabani Mligo proves that Africans have a religion besides the denial of some Western scholars in regard to this fact. When attempting to discuss about African religion, Mligo has provided some details of rich African practices that are part and parcel of African Religion. He also emphasizes on the African concept of God while many scholars from the West deny it. For them, Africans still worship gods and not the One Supreme God. Mligo provides a proof of the existence of the concept of God in African Traditional Religion before the coming of missionaries by narrating the way Africans perceived the existence of God through various attributes such as: unknowable nature of God, omnipotence, Holiness, kindness, spiritual nature, everlastingness, etc.

Mligo's work challenges African scholars who belong to the new generation to carry out researches on this religion which has been disregarded by comparative religionists for so long a time. He insists that the research on African religion should be conducted by Africans themselves who are part of the community, think like them, feel like them, and experience life like them. Of cause, Mligo's argument does not mean that the study should be done by African scholars alone; he most likely means that whoever intends to do a research on elements of African Traditional Religion must be fully committed to the perspective of the African natives leaving behind all erroneous pre-conceived notions. Such a person is obliged to be closer with Africans and be part of them. In other words, such a person should always take an emic perspective in his/her approach to research.

In this book, Mligo through his chapter four provides new insights by emphasizing that a study of African Traditional Religion is not a study about old and outdated practices. Instead, it is a study about the living religion and practices of African people. Mligo has illustrated this fact through the examples of worship services, sacrifices, and symbolism at Nyumbanitu worship shrine among the Bena of Njombe (and surrounding ethnic groups) in Tanzania and other places of Africa. Therefore, these illustrations indicate that the person studying African Traditional Religion is not supposed to go to the museum or huge library in order to acquire the required data, but to just live with community members and experience their daily life.

To my judgment, Mligo's work "*Elements of African Traditional Religion*" is not a new discovery. Instead, it is a new reflection of the old discovery, a reflection that fits to the present context. Most of the books about African religion and practice used by students in universities and colleges within and outside Africa have been written by Western authors. In such cases, students have greatly lacked African flavor. For this purpose, as some other African scholars have done, Mligo's book seems to have greatly considered the African audience. However, the book has not left aside the Western audience; instead, the content of the book can possibly enlighten them. Therefore, the book can serve as a proper resource for students doing comparative religions and scholars teaching this subject. It can also be of great help to all people who want to acquire a general

Foreword

knowledge of African religion and practices within and outside Africa.

The language used in this work is simplified for readers of all calibers: those whose English language is first, second, third or whatever. Moreover, Mligo has provided enough examples from Nyumbanitu worship shrine that make the content of the book live, clear, contextual, and understandable. These examples and a simplified language he uses make the book not only serve for the two purposes mentioned above, but also provide fruitful inspiration to young people to do researches on various topics from African religion and practice. The book can also be the basis for knowledge about globalization and the place of African Religion in African context in relation to the other world religions. For this matter, it should be clear that Africans can hardly understand globalization if they do not clearly know their African religious background.

Falres Ipyana Ilomo
Lecturer in Missiology and Religions
University of Iringa, Tanzania
12 May 2013

Acknowledgments

A BOOK PROJECT IS a corporate work of many contributors, each one participating according to his/her own part. This has been the case for this book. I appreciate the contribution of many people towards the form that this book has at the moment. More specifically, I appreciate the contribution of my colleagues at Amani University Project in Njombe and the Faculty of Theology at The University of Iringa for their constructive criticisms in discussions of the various drafts of the book manuscript. More specifically, I am indebted to my two research assistants: Innocent Pius Kibadu and Stanley Nicolaus Kambo for their commitment in research work; and to Farles Ipyana Ilomo for commenting on the second draft of my book manuscript and writing the foreword. Moreover, I am indebted to Bupe Nelson Nyakule, the Personal Secretary at Amani University Project, for typing the book manuscript in the computer.

I am also grateful to the two priests of Nyumbanitu Bena worship shrine in Njombe (Alex Vangimeli Msigwa and Julius Vangimeli Msigwa) for teaching me the traditions and heritages of my ancestors preserved at Nyumbanitu. Their information was of great importance to make this book live and substantial. I dedicate this book to this valuable and enormous worship shrine as a memory of my study visit.

Acknowledgments

I do not forget my editors at Wipf and Stock who accepted my book manuscript, polished it, and made it readable. Their work is excellent and appreciable. Last, but not least, my wife Ester and our three children, Upendo, Grace, and Faraja for being able to tolerate and pray for the academically busy and unavailable father like me. May the Lord God grant you peace of mind and thoughtful life?

Peculiar Features of African Traditional Religion

It is a religion that is mainly based on oral transmission from one generation to another. Its teachings are not written on paper, but in the hearts, minds, oral history, rituals, shrines, and religious functions of people who believe in and practice this religion.

It is a religion that has no founder as it is in other major world religions: Islam (Muhammad), Christianity (Jesus Christ), Buddhism (Gautama the Buddha), etc. This religion does not hail one religious hero; but, it is an inborn and lived in the whole life of the ones embracing it.

It is not a missionary religion, and neither does it have missionaries to propagate it or even make converts through a certain ritual. Adherents become members not by a ritual (like baptism, or circumcision) but by birth.

1

Introduction

CURRENT CONCERNS ABOUT AFRICAN TRADITIONAL RELIGION

AFRICAN TRADITIONAL RELIGION is the region of the indigenous people in Africa. It is the way in which indigenous people relate to the Supreme Being in their own context. However, some Africans may still ask: Why should they study African Traditional Religion at this age whereby globalization makes all truth claims relative and raises doubts to all beliefs and practices taken for granted by human societies? Some church or religious workers may still ask: What is the use of African Traditional Religion at their age whereby most people are Christians baptized in the name of the Holy Trinity, Muslims well Islamized, Hindus, Shintos or Buddhists? What is it for? These workers may further claim: "We need to be current and up-to-date". They may assert that African Traditional Religion is just a passing phenomenon (i.e., it is *zilipendwa*), much more traditional,

Elements of African Traditional Religion

and is irrelevant to their understanding of the present younger generation.

Others may still say: African Traditional Religion is irrelevant to the current twenty-first century, a century of science and technology. Some questions may further be asked: What is the relevance of this religion at this age whereby people are longing towards the discoveries of new phenomena? Is there a chief benefit of African Traditional Religion to this globalized generation whereby the heterogeneity of word cultures are now being homogenized into one super culture? If there is, is it a benefit related to the knowledge of history of the way our ancestors once lived with their own cultural values?[1] However, whether we like it or not, we need to know African Traditional Religion in order to understand and minister in the post-independent Africa.

We learn African Traditional Religion in order to understand our context as Africans and to understand the new religion (Christianity or any other) that comes into our soil and minister it well in our African Context. This means that the knowledge of African Traditional Religion is the most important aspect in Africa. This knowledge leads us to the understanding of our *life* and *culture*. By culture, here I mean the "sum total of all people's traditional religions, customs, traditions, rites, ceremonies, symbols, art, wisdom and institutions . . . the way they relate to the Supreme Being, to the supernatural powers and phenomena, to their fellowmen and women, to the world of other living beings and inanimate beings, and to the world underground."[2]

The above definition indicates that culture is the mirror of ones life. If one understands his/her culture well, he/she will also understand life. When we turn back and look at the past, how our ancestors lived, we understand their

1. Gehman, *African Traditional Religion*, 15.
2. Walligo, "Making the Church," 27.

Introduction

general life which enlightens ours. No one of us living in the present time can know of his/her life well without first understanding the life of his/her past parents. This means that culture and life are totally inseparable. When one understands culture he/she understands life and vice versa. This culture is not something static but something dynamic. The culture of the parents is passed to the lives of the younger generations.

Culture also includes Religion. To force people to abandon religion, as some missionaries did when they just came to Africa, is to try forcing them to abandon their culture. Since culture includes the whole life of a person and his/her community, converting a person to another culture is taking that person away from his/her life. This was what missionaries tried to force people from their religion towards another religion—Christianity; hence, leading them to the production of innumerable half-Christians.[3]

African Traditional Religion is the religion for the whole Africa, as Christianity is now becoming a religion for most people of the world. For the sake of Christians, we need to study African Traditional Religion in order to understand what it offers us towards the better understanding of the Bible in our own context. This will be possible through studying people's traditional cultures. Through a careful and serious study of the people's local traditional cultures, Christians have "to discover those fundamental elements that must be purified, those which need substitutes, those which have to be rejected without a substitute and those which can be incorporated in Christianity without any change."[4]

---

3. Gichure, "Religion and Politics," 34–35.
4. Walligo, "Making the Church," 28.

Elements of African Traditional Religion

WHY SHOULD WE STUDY AFRICAN TRADITIONAL RELIGION?

After stating the questions of people's current concerns for the need of African Traditional Religion and the need for understanding the cultural backgrounds of our ancestors, let us now focus, in a more detail, on the basic question: Why should we study African Traditional Religion at this time whereby modern religions, such as Christianity, are more resurgent and well-received by people? Some of the reasons I propose are the following:

First, African Traditional Religion is one of the world religions with great people and great past. When I emphasize that African Traditional Religion is a religion with great people I mean that African Traditional Religion is not a religion embraced by only one person, tribe, clan, or country. It is a religion of the whole continent of Africa with regardless of the diversity of its people. It is also embraced by African people that are outside Africa such as Haiti, United States of Africa and South America. This means that wherever the African is, it is where his/her religion is.

When I say that it is a religion with great past I mean that the religion is as ancient as the African people themselves. As Chepkwony writes, "African Religion is as old as Africans themselves, and as archeological findings have shown, the African continent is probably the cradle of humanity. Like all the people of the world, Africa has a long history albeit unwritten."[5] Hence, African Traditional Religion forms the culture of the people and the way they live and understand the world around them. The historicity of African religion is not written in documents; but, as Mbiti

---

5. Chepkwony, "African Religion," 41, cf. All Africa Conference of Churches, *Problems and Promises*, 56–57.

Introduction

asserts, it "is written in the history, the hearts and experiences of the people."[6]

However, comparative religionists have exerted great exclusions of African Traditional Religion in the academic arena as a world religion despite its long historical background. Their major arguments are mainly based on the comparability of African Traditional Religion in relation to other world religions. It has been argued that African Traditional Religion has no founders, temples, history, written book, revelation, etc. As Adam K. A. Chepkwony states: "The comparative religionists have, however, accepted Hinduism, Buddhism, Jainism, Confucianism, Taoism, Shintoism, Zoroastrianism, Judaism, Christianity, Islam and Sikhism as world religions."[7] On the bases of the comparability of African Traditional Religion with the named world religions, none of the scholars of the History of Religion has dared to venture into dealing with African Religion since the study of the history of religion started within the western world in the second half of the nineteenth century.[8]

Nevertheless, this exclusion of African Traditional Religion in the academic arena indicates the way the study of comparative religion has been superficial because it has not taken seriously the religion of the African masses. As Chepkwony affirms, "the History of Religion should include all religions of humankind."[9] Hence, we need to study African Traditional Religion in the academic arena in order to enhance a better comparative study of all major world religions, including African Traditional Religion.

---

6. Mbiti, *Introduction to African Religion*, Second Edition, 5; cf. King, *African Cosmos*, 1–2.

7. Chepkwony, "African Religion," 30, cf. Ibid., 37–39.

8. Ibid.

9. Ibid., 31.

Elements of African Traditional Religion

Moreover, theologian Laurenti Magesa further emphasizes: "The tendency of some philosophers, theologians and students of comparative religion is still to regard African Religion as a 'primal' or 'ethnic' religion, thus robbing it of its universal character."[10] He adds: "The attitude also reduces the capability of African religion to interact with other religions and to influence and change the world and minimizes its role in conversation with other religions."[11] According to Magesa, this attitude develops because of the spirit of superiority that dominated the nineteenth century missionaries who considered African Traditional Religion as barbarous, fetish, and childish.[12]

In fact, this kind of consideration of African Traditional Religion is just a prejudice because it lacks a sensible justification of its claim; and neither does it hold any powerful truth today. Considering African Traditional Religion as tribal, fetish, barbarous, and whatever pejorative name may be applied is actually considering all religions in that way. This is because all religions have an essence and a culture. Christianity begun as a sect within Judaism in the Middle East and was considered pejoratively by other surrounding religions (including Judaism itself), and so do all world religions. This means that a pejorative consideration of a religion is mainly due to ignorance of what encompasses that religion.[13]

Jean Holm provides us an important warning about the way one should approach other people's religions. In the Preface of the book Women in Religion, he begins by these exciting words: "The person who knows only one religion

---

10. Magesa, *African Religion*, 28.
11. Ibid.
12. Ibid.
13. Ibid.

does not know any religion."[14] In this statement, Holm tries to point out the diversity of religious beliefs and claims for truth and "how mistaken are those who assume that the pattern of belief and practice in their own religion is reflected equally in other religions."[15] Holm points out that drawing a line between religions and confining truths within them is doing injustices to such religions because such religions do not exist in a vacuum. He further writes, "Religions don't exist in a vacuum; they are influenced by the social and cultural contexts in which they are set. This can affect what they strenuously reject as well as what they may absorb into their pattern of belief and practice."[16] Hence, Holm's statements above indicate that every religion has autonomy and holds truth to those who embrace it. A person approaching such religions needs to do it with a positive attitude to them instead of seeing them as heathen as the missionaries did to African Traditional Religion.

Second, there is a need to study African Traditional Religion if Christianity has to be meaningful to African context now. We need to bridge the gap between the world of Christianity and the world of the African people that is mostly shaped by the African Traditional Religion. This learning will make it possible to evangelize Africans at their own context. Understanding African Traditional Religion is needed because the evangelization of the African people needs to start from the known to the unknown. African Traditional Religion is known by African people while Christianity is foreign. Therefore, we study it in order to make people disciples of Christ in an African context through better contextualization of the gospel message.

14. Holm, "Preface," vi.
15. Ibid.
16. Ibid.

Elements of African Traditional Religion

However, this evangelization is not of just proselytizing Africans to Christianity as it was prior conceived by the early missionaries. It is of preparing the grounds for mutual dialogue between the known African Traditional Religious faith and practices and the unknown Christian faith and practices. In fact, dialogue is the manner of bearing witness to one's own held truth, with sympathy and readiness to listen to the dialogue partner's own witness. It is reciprocity of witnesses mutually shared between two partners; it is a conversation that makes the exchange of ideas between two persons possible. The aim of dialogue is always to learn from each other. This means that dialogue is not tied by one's wish to convert, proselytize, or claim the possession of absolute truth upon the dialoguing partner. Therefore, through understanding African Traditional Religion, the dialogue between the two religions will be possible because "African Religion and culture forms the context, or the root paradigm, for interpreting the Christian message from the socio-cultural and historical experiences of the African peoples."[17]

Third, the problems about the concept of God in African Traditional Religion must be cleared. The coming of Christianity brought a new impetus towards what people believed and practiced in African Traditional Religion. As a matter of fact, the belief in the Supreme Being in African Traditional Religion was also distorted. Some Christians claimed, and still claim, that African Traditional Religion has no good understanding of God. These Christians say that African Traditional Religion is Satanic, and through this understanding, some Christian theologians and lay people are reluctant to study African Traditional Religion. However, most of these people who come for baptism and who attend the church (more than 50%) still attend

17. Chepkwony, "African Religion," 30, cf. Sundermeier, *The Individual and the Community*, 233–240.

Introduction

and think of African Traditional Religion. They practice "religious concubinage"[18], that is, they have two faiths at a go. In this case, as Walligo quoting R. Gray and F. Luke writes, Christians "find themselves divided into two personalities, one African and the other Christian. During the time of joy and peace they may be able to live as true Christians, but when crises come, whether of illness, suffering misfortune, death, barrenness and so on, they easily, move back to their African personality and engage in ceremonies, rites and world view that have been constantly condemned by the church."[19]

Religious concubinage has been expressed with different tones by different African scholars who try to show the outcome of not taking the indigenous people's culture seriously. I. K. Katoke argues that the coming of missionaries and their neglect of the existing culture produced "half-converted" Christians who were "half-cultures." What type of Christians were these? According to Katoke, these were Christians who partly believed in Christianity and partly in their traditional religion. They were Christians who adhered to Christianity because of gaining favors from it but their mind and real obedience was paid to their traditional religion. Katoke states thus: "Some of these 'half-converted' hung on to it or retained the new names because by remaining a Christian one was assured of getting a job in the

---

18. The term "concubinage" has its counterpart term "syncretism." While concubinage refers to one having or embracing two incompatible faiths without combining and reconciling the two, syncretism on the other hand refers to one embracing two faiths and reconciling them so as to become one faith from the two incompatible faiths. For further elaboration on the concept of syncretism see Gehman, *African Traditional Religion*, 270–273; Schreiter, *Constructing Local Theologies*, 144–158; Schreiter, *The New Catholicity*, 62–83.

19. Walligo, "Making the Church," 22, cf. Gichure, "Religion and politics," 35.

services of the church or colonial administration—which carried substantial salary. Moreover being a Christian was a sign of being 'civilized' at least in the eyes of westerners."[20] Therefore, concubinage carries with it a wider perspective trying to explain why Christianity has remained foreign throughout the ages since it was implanted in an African soil. During the time of joy, people are Christians, but during the time of problems like sickness, deaths, etc., people turn to their traditional diviners.

Following the description above, the question is: Why do these people, whatever name we may call them religious concubines, half-Christians, half-backed Christians, half-converted Christians, etc., consult diviners in search for the causes of their problems while they know for sure that they have numerous biomedical laboratories around them and some pastors in their churches whom they ought to consult during their times of crises? Is their action sinful or not? Why? The possible answer to these questions bases on the type of service these laboratory facilities and pastors provide to their respective Christian clients when consulted. Perhaps these laboratory facilities and pastors provide inadequate answers to their day to day problems facing them religiously, socially and economically.

Another question is this: Does the Christian Scripture speak to the problems facing African Christians today? In order to answer this question, we need to have a thorough knowledge of African Traditional Religion and its values and beliefs that characterize the people's lived context. The Christian church in Africa needs to contextualize her faith in order that it becomes truly rooted in the lives of the people. Scholars use various terms to try express on the manner of expression and communication of the gospel faith to a different culture from the original culture of

20. Katoke, "The Coming of the Gospel," 110.

Introduction

the Bible. The terms such as: inculturation, indigenization, reformation, incarnation and interculturation have been used.[21] This means that the manner of communication and expression of the gospel faith varies from people to people, even the manner of worship differs greatly among people in the world.

Grebe and Fon provide us an example in the area of Christian counseling that illustrate the need to understand and practice Christianity in the context of the people being served. They write: "The Christian counselor needs to know intimately the worldview of the counselee, in order to understand his [sic!] problems and temptations. Furthermore he needs to have a clear grasp of the essentials of ATR and to have interpreted them in light of Scriptures, so that he knows what the strongholds of Satan in ATR are that need to be broken down. He needs to know what are neutral cultural aspects, or even elements of truth, that he can build on in guiding the counselee to biblical solutions."[22] This statement cements on the need to understand African Traditional Religion before doing the Christian social practices among people.

However, the gospel itself is unchanging. It remains the same; that is, the gospel remains unchanged. This means that in the communication of this unchanged message, the formalized ecclesiastical expression of faith should have indelible marks of particular people. To be sure, there are biblical guidelines but not biblical formulae that are inflexible and uniform for every culture. The Bible provides out some guidelines to contextualize its message without diluting the message itself.

---

21. See Walligo, "Making the Church," 11–12 for the meaning and usage of the term.

22. Grebe & Fon, "African Traditional Religion," 93–94.

Elements of African Traditional Religion

It is open and known, that the Holy Spirit stamps to everyone with the mark of divine life. However, this life then reflects the cultural diversity of the people. Today, because of this cultural diversity, there is a cry throughout Africa for the genuine African authentic Christianity, which is truly rooted in the life of the indigenous people. This cry means that the gospel needs to be communicated in culturally relevant ways which can be understood by African people. The gospel must come alive to people by clothing it, or emanating from the African culture and African people's ways of life.

When missionaries came to the African continent, they came with the gospel (message) clothed with their own clothes (cultures). African people got confused by the message they received because it was clothed with a foreign culture. This means that there is a great need to contextualize the gospel message in the African culture itself without distorting this message.

African people are essentially the same, embracing the same culture despite the various minor tribal cultural differences. They have the same religion despite the various denominations embraced by tribal and clan religious practices. Hence, the gospel message needs to emanate from the lived experiences of African people as they use the biblical guidelines to discern this message. African people must take the unchanging message of the Bible and see how that message can illuminate indigenous African people in the development of theology from their lived contexts. This indigenous theology is expected to emanate from people's particular needs; and hence, it should be an African Christian Theology.

For all these to happen, we need to know the context of African Christianity. This context includes African Traditional Religion. African Traditional Religion is a native religion, a home religion of the Africans. It is not a religion imposed to people through evangelization as Christianity

Introduction

is. The problem is not to Christianity as a religion, but to the vehicles (i.e., the missionaries) of this religion. Which factors did they consider when imposing it to people of a different culture from their own?

FACTORS TO CONSIDER IN THE STUDY OF AFRICAN TRADITIONAL RELIGION

The most important factor is that of objectivity. We need to understand that before 19th and 20th centuries, there was no objectivity. People studied things as they appeared to them and truth was considered to be absolute. When people studied things as they were, misrepresentations were inevitable. African Traditional Religion subjectively may lead to reading in African Traditional Religion what is not there, or reading out from African Traditional Religion what is not indigenous. In this case, an objective approach is necessary and important in approaching African Traditional Religion.

Bolaji Idowu clearly states: "You can approach the study of African Traditional Religion without any preconceived notion." You study starting with an empty head. Idowu sympathizes with the World Council of Churches slogan that "The world should provide its agenda". Here it means that someone has to approach the study of African Traditional Religion with no agenda.

However, Gehman contends that "It is humanly impossible. Every man has his humanly preconceived ideas when he starts studying something."[23] Gehman might be right in his point, but both points above, may have some sort of reality. What we need to emphasize here is that when entering the study of African Traditional Religion the stu-

23. Gehman, African *Traditional Religion* (1986).

dents need to limit their preconceived presuppositions as much as possible.

Most African theologians contend that many books are written concerning African Traditional Religion. However, there are few among those books that aim at developing African Traditional Religion in a Christian perspective. Moreover, many of then are written without considering objectivity, i.e., they write with pre-conceived notions or ideas about African Traditional Religion. In such books, African Traditional Religion is not colored by African cultural and religious perspectives, but by foreign culture, expressions, and foreign understanding.

PRELIMINARY UNDERSTANDING OF RELIGION

Throughout history, religion has been a central part of human experience; it has been a part in which people perceive and react to their environment in which they live. What provides room for this perception and reaction is *Experience*. In analyzing religious practices or studying religious experiences we need to bear in mind that there are many religious beliefs and rituals found in various human cultures. We need to recognize the diversity of religions as a general phenomenon. This means that without considering religion as a phenomenon it becomes difficult to try expressing it.

The first attempt we have to do is to try defining religion. It is not easy to have a single straightforward definition of religion. As Nyaundi writes, "Religion is a multi-dimensional concept because it is many things to many people. What is called religion to one society is often times different from what another society would call religion."[24] How-

24. Gichure, "Religion and Politics in Africa," 36.

Introduction

ever, Kenneth Cragg, quoting Walt Whitman, compares the enigma found in defining music with that of defining religion. Cragg says thus: "'All music is what awakes from you when you are reminded by the instrument.' (. . .). Religion, like music, is hard to define. Both live in the interplay of soul and significance, of reality akin and yet beyond ourselves, of meaning in its own right and of response in ours. Worship is just such an awakening to relationship amid reminders that surround us everywhere."[25] Gichure in his article "Religion and Politics in Africa" attempts a definition similar to Cragg's explanations above. For him, "Religion can be defined as 'the human response to reality. Ideally religion expresses the spirituality of a people in terms of creeds, cults, code of conduct and a confessional community.'"[26] The difficulty pinpointed by Cragg above and the unsatisfactory attempt made by Gichure indicate to us that in order to properly approach the concept of 'religion' more adequately we have to start on the side of what religion is not:

1. Religion should not be identified with monotheism. Monotheism confines religion to those religions that believe only on the unity of God, i.e., that have faith in one God.

2. Religion should not be identified with certain moral prescriptions (cf. the difficulty of the philosophical question of determining what is right and what is wrong).

3. Religion is not necessarily concerned with explaining how the world came into being. The description provided by religion about the way the world came into being is just a small part of what constitutes religion.

25. Cragg, *The Christian*, 31.
26. Gichure, "Religion and Politics," 37.

Elements of African Traditional Religion

4. Religion cannot be identified with the Supernatural Powers, an identification which involves the belief in the universe, etc. All these are just parts of aspects that contribute to what religion really means, but they are not the sole aspects without which religion cannot be conceived.

After this attempt we move towards clarifying, what religion likely is: Here we concentrate on the following characteristics of religion.[27]

1. Religion involves a set of beliefs: whether beliefs in God, ideology, a big tree, a big stone, a huge forest, a mountain, etc. It is not only one belief, but a set of beliefs that make up of a system of interaction individuals in a particular society have with the Supreme Being

2. Religion involves a set of symbols that explain the reality beyond what is seen, e.g., church, cross, mosque, moon and star, temple, etc. Symbols have meaning in them. They communicate to adherents of a particular religion something beyond what is seen and believed.

3. Religion involves invoking feelings about rituals, harvesting ceremonies, Sunday or Friday worships, wedding ceremonies, etc. Ceremonies make the actualization of meaning about a particular event possible. For example, in Christianity the Sunday worship done repeatedly in every Sunday actualizes the resurrection of Christ which is one of the major teachings of the Christian religion.

There are many theories about religion and its origin. In order to examine the validity of African Traditional Religion as a religion we survey the following four of these theories:

27. Cf. Brown, *A Guide to Religions*, 8.

Introduction

1. Feuerbach (1804–1872)—Feuerbach developed an "anthropological essence of religion" in his book *The Essence of Christianity* (1841). Feuerbach believed that Religion consists of ideas and values produced by human beings in the course of their cultural development, but mistakenly or unfortunately, projected on divine forces or God. The idea is that Religion consists of ideas produced by a human being from his/her cultural development. Therefore, Feuerbach limits religion to the sphere of society.

According to him, religion is man-centered (i.e., anthropocentric) and it is an outward projection of the human being's nature dwelling in him/her. Though human beings stand at the centre of religion, according to the definition projected above, yet religion is not religion only because of human beings that embrace a particular religion. Religion is religion because it embraces more than the human being that embraces it. Religion includes the relationship between human beings, the symbols and the Supreme Being venerated and worshipped. How does African Traditional Religion fit in this theory? Is African Traditional Religion anthropocentric having some ideas forged in by human beings? In fact, though African Traditional Religion cannot reflect what exactly Feuerbach spells out, yet it consists most of his ideas.

2. Karl Marx (1818–1883)—Max links religion with materialism—his social economic philosophy. He states that religion represents human alienation. Religion is the heart of heartless world, a heaven from the harshness of the daily reality. Religion in its traditional form, according to Marx, will ultimately disappear because it is false, and is linked to human exploitation. It creates a false consciousness among people which justifies their silent exploitation.

According to Marx, the more religion creates a false consciousness to people, the more it provides hope, it

Elements of African Traditional Religion

provides a false hope that creates irresponsibility to adherents of that religion in regard to the existing economic situation. Max saw religion to be 'opium of the people' because it prohibited social change by prohibiting resistance to oppression. True hope and true happiness, according to Max, comes only through revolution against economically oppressive structures that create classes among society members.

One of the weaknesses of Maxist view of religion is its view of religion as a weapon of the ruling class to impart ideologies that make people patiently accept the exploitative systems, a thing that is against the definition of religion provided above.[28] Is African Traditional Religion a false religion because it provides a false consciousness among African people to silence them from facing the reality of their situation as Marx observes? In fact, African Traditional Religion is clear about the weakness of Marx's theory of religion stated above. African Traditional Religion is not a religion of only providing hope to African people; but, it is a life-lived culture whereby a person is born and incorporated into the rhythms of this religion. This means that African Traditional Religion belongs to the whole community and none of the community members uses it as a weapon over against other people for his/her own purpose as Marx conceives of religion.

3. **Emil Durkheim (1858–1917)**—Durkheim understands religion in terms of the sacred and the profane. He emphasizes that Religion is defined and understood in terms of the distinction between sacred and secular. Some religions have sacred objects or symbols (totem) and secular. This means that "the distinction between sacred and profane is found in all religions and is the fundamental

---

28. Kunin, "Anthropological and Sociological Theories," 64–67.

characteristic of religious thought."[29] According to him, religion is holy, and this is a Western understanding. But the idea behind is that when talking of religion in Western understanding it is both sacred and secular. The object of worship, according to him is the society itself. Durkheim strongly emphasizes that regular ceremonies and ritual activities, measure religion in terms of its ability to answer people's basic needs of the society. In this case, the society is viewed by Durkheim as God because of the resurgence and influence of civil celebrations such as parades, and people's strong patriotic adherence that seem to him to promote what he calls '*civil religion.*'

However, the weakness of Durkheims theory of religion is that it overemphasizes the social nature of religion and forgets the individual part of it. This means that religion is both individual and social experience of reality.[30] Kunin emphasizes: "Although Durkheim's emphasis on society and the social construction of the individual is a very important building block in the understanding of religion and society, it does, perhaps to too great an extent, devalue the importance of the individual as a mediator for social facts. Social facts do shape the individual but he or she equally shapes them through the practice of the social facts."[31] Moreover, Durkheim believed in science and the growth of modernity. For him, this growth of modernity and science could replace religion by reducing its influence to society as it modernizes.

Durkheim's emphasis on society is much more similar to the emphasis of African Traditional Religion on community. It is an emphasis of African Traditional Religion that religion belongs to the community. The practice of

29. Ibid., 74.
30. Ibid.
31. Ibid., 76.

Elements of African Traditional Religion

African Traditional Religion is primarily communal before it becomes individual. As the emphasis on society is the weakness for Durkheim's theory, it is more likely the strength and weakness of African Traditional Religion that emphasizes more on community than the individual adherents. The emphasis on community is strength to African Traditional Religion because communal life is the bases for both life and religion in African perspective. It is a weakness because despite the communal life, there is still an individual and his/her own experience of the life and religion that also needs to be taken seriously.

However, the difference between Durkheim's theory and African Traditional Religion's views is that African Traditional Religion does not differentiate between the secular and sacred. All aspects are united together in African Traditional Religion. Therefore, African Traditional Religion embraces some peculiar aspects that can hardly be in keeping with Durkheim's theoretical perspectives.

4. African Traditional Religious Theory—In the conception of African worldview, religion is experienced as a response to all life in the world in relation to the Supreme Being (*God*). This means that Africans seem to be instinctively religious in their own way, and according to their own ideas. Religion is one of their lives, a life-lived religiously. It is a religious life which absorbs the whole man, which is identified with them, with their thoughts and actions. Therefore, according to the theory of African Traditional Religion, religion is people's whole lives in relation to the Supreme Being, and in relation to one another within their community.

In summary we can say that religion is seen more clearly as a life-lived aspect. It is inseparable from the person's life and appears between the spiritual and the material aspects of that person. Religion is not merely a religious

Introduction

system with creeds, with moral codes, or with an honoured liturgy, etc. Rather, religion is an institution in which one has the whole of his/her life. In general, therefore, in African Traditional Religion, religion is the whole life of an African in relation to God.

NATURAL SETTING AND PERSPECTIVES ON AFRICAN TRADITIONAL RELIGION

When we turn to looking at the setting and perspectives of African Traditional Religion, we want to concentrate more on the two major views of African Traditional Religion: The old and the new views of African Traditional Religion. The old view portrays the way in which African Traditional Religion has been misunderstood, and the modern view tries to correct the misconceptions.

Old View of African Traditional Religion

It is true to say that African Traditional Religion has been more misunderstood and has suffered more jeopardizing language at the hand of the early writers than any other part of literature relating to human life. It is unhappy to us that the Old View through its old misconceptions provides us with vague understanding of religion (ATR) until today. The way the early writers understood African Traditional Religious rites, rituals, symbols, etc., indicate that such writers were ignorant of what Africans were doing according to their cultural backgrounds. Some of these misconceptions include the following:

(i) Identifying African Traditional Religion with the worship of the false gods (Bosman in the 18th century)

Elements of African Traditional Religion

    (ii) Affiliating African Traditional Religious beliefs with illogical beliefs (Barton, ca. 1864)

    (iii) Conceiving that Africans have no belief in any Supreme Being (Baker—ca. 1867 in Sudan)

These are some of such misconceptions about African Traditional Religion. However, all of them are mostly based on a subjective approach to African Traditional Religion. Most of those who pronounced about African Traditional Religion were Western scholars. For them, African Traditional Religion did not resemble what they embraced at their context, which they considered as being correct and true.

Modern View of African Traditional Religion

African scholar Bolaji Idowu writes: Religion cannot be studied properly unless it is studied from the inside not from the outside. Those who are prepared to enter into the feeling of worshippers and to sit where they sit are the ones who can properly study the worshippers' religion. If these are done, a proper study of African Traditional Religion will be done. To enter into their feelings is to sympathize with them and what they believe and practice.

    What Idowu means in the above assertion is that each religion must be seen in its own perspective and dimension, not in another religion's dimensions; otherwise, the studied religion cannot be without some pre-conceived notions. And if not possible, the preconceived notions should not be criteria for the study. The student of African Traditional Religion needs to leave the actual situation to provide the agenda. In other words, the student needs to leave the religion to reveal itself. The necessary passport into that sacred country of study is the "imaginative sympathy and readiness to learn." In doing that the student or scholar will

Introduction

be trying to enter into the feelings of the people and seeing with his/her eyes in order to understand what actually people in that country believe and practice.

From this background, many people in Africa have started to believe anew. African people have started to think of their religion as the one that worship the same God as that of Christianity and Islam. It is not the worship of idols as it was thought in the old view. However, there are still some people who try to claim that African Traditional Religion cannot be compared with higher Religions, e.g., Christianity, Islam, Buddhism, etc. because it has no recognized *long history*, that it has no *extensive sacred writings*, that it has no *temples and liturgy*, and that it has no priests. In fact all these claims are not at all reasonable enough to dismiss African Traditional Religion to the reputation held by higher religions.

The fact that African Traditional Religion has no written history does not mean that African Traditional Religion has no long history. Even in higher religions written materials came later, but history started before. In Christianity, for example, the written, materials of the Bible are said to have been collected from oral traditions which were the beginning of history.

Some scholars have reached a point of believing that since African Traditional Religion does not have most of the above characteristics, it is a primitive religion. This way of looking at African Traditional Religion does not also hold any water. Africa itself must show the way it started and developed not other people from abroad. However, African Traditional Religion is not a *bookish religion*. Chapters of African Traditional Religion are written everywhere in the community and are available to everyone to be read. Mbiti is quite clear about this notion when he writes that African

Elements of African Traditional Religion

Traditional Religion "is a living religion which is written in the lives of the people."[32]

In fact, as Healey and Zybertz put it, the "African Oral theology is a living reality. We must come to terms with it. We must acknowledge its role (. . .). It is the most articulated expression of theological creativity in Africa."[33] The words of Healey and Zybertz above imply that African Traditional values are transmitted orally from one generation to another. It is a lived-reality whereby an African is incorporated as is born and grows. Andrew A. Kyomo emphasizes thus in regard to the transmission of African oral traditions: "In African religion, the term 'oral tradition' refers not only to oral transmission of tradition but also to the content of what is transmitted—a world view and a way of life. African oral tradition asserts that there is a Supreme Being who is the source of life and makes life itself meaningful."[34]

Kyomo further notes: "AR has no written scriptures like Hinduism, Judaism, Islam or Christianity. It survives and will continue to survive without sacred writings. Why? The answer is that it is communicated holistically. The faith of an indigenous African is a 'revealed' one from the Supreme Being through the ancestors."[35] Hinduism has the Upanishads as its scripture; Islam has the Qur'an; Buddhism has the Thammapada; Judaism has the Old Testament, and Christianity has the Old and New Testaments; but African Traditional Religion has no written scripture. More emphasis has been made by Laurent Magesa in his book *African Religion: The Moral Traditions of Abundant Life* (1997). Magesa, as quoted by Kyomo, writes: "For Africans, religion is far more

32. Mbiti, *Introduction to African Religion*, Second Edition, 131.
33. Healey & Zybertz, *Towards an African Narrative Theology*, 22.
34. Kyomo, "Oral Tradition," 75.
35. Ibid, 79.

Introduction

than 'a believing way of life' or 'an approach to life' directed by a book. It is a way of life' or life itself, where a distinction or separation is not made between religion and other areas of human existence."[36] The contributions of the above scholars indicate that a book is not a prerequisite for a religion to be religion in its general sense. Belief systems, symbolic meanings and practices, and the way such systems are transmitted from one generation to another within a particular society are important aspects for a religion.

Concerning the religiosity of the Africans, John S. Mbiti puts it this way: "Wherever the African is, there is his religion; he carries crop; he takes it with him to the beer party or to attend a funeral ceremony (. . .) to the house of parliament (. . .) everybody is a religious carrier. So then, belief and act in African Traditional Society cannot be separated; they belong to a single whole."[37] What Mbiti asserts in the above statements is that Africans are religious people. Their religiosity does not mainly depend on a book as other higher religions are. Every person has a religious system found in the whole of his/her life. It is not easy to separate this religious system with the entire life of the African person.

It is in the above perspective of understanding African Traditional Religion that makes it important in the life of the African people. African theologian Maurice M. Makumba in his book *Introduction to African Philosophy*

---

36. Ibid., cf. Gichure, "Religion and Politics," 34–35. Theo Sundermeier futher notes that African Traditional Religion is the '*Primary religious experience*' whereby the entrance of onother religions in an African soil constitutes a '*Secondary experience*.' According to him, "Secondary religious experience does not simply replace the primary once for all. It is premised on primary experience, which provides the presuppositions for understanding the new."(Sundermeier, *The Individual and the Community*, 236).

37. Mbiti, *Concepts of God*, 2.

Elements of African Traditional Religion

emphasizes the importance of African Traditional Religion to the lives of people when he writes: "Another important characteristic of most African societies is the role of religion in the lives of the people. Religion was not conceived of as a mere profession of a creed coming at some defined time in the person's life, but rather as being part and parcel of one's way of living. It was difficult (not impossible) to think of a religion-less individual, as difficult as it was to think of an ethics-less person (even if the possibility of the existence of such people still remains). One was born into a religious atmosphere, lived religiously and went to join the ancestors in a religious way."[38] This means that every member of African society is faithful to his/her own religion into which he/she was born.

When we talk of African religions (denominations) we refer to the African people each having a particular own religious system. To ignore these traditional beliefs and practices can lead to the lack of understanding of African behavior and African problems. This clearly means that religion in Africa is the strongest element in the African people's background and provides considerable influence to their thinking and practice.

What does the above description imply to us and our current understanding of African Traditional Religion as compared to the claims against African Traditional Religion in relation to other higher religions? This description implies that even after Christianity, African Traditional Religion continued to have influence to the converted Christians because African Traditional Religion is part and parcel of their lives and Christianity was foreign religion to them. Wherever the African is, there is his/her religion. Religion is not limited to temples, churches and priests. Hence, in the African society, there are no irreligious people. This means that for someone

38. Makumba, *Introduction to African Philosophy*, 129.

Introduction

to claim as being irreligious is to excommunicate oneself from the entire life of the African community.

FURTHER AFRICAN PERSPECTIVES ON AFRICAN TRADITIONAL RELIGION

There is no word "Religion" in Africa and in Kiswahili in particular, the language used by most nations belonging to the eastern part of Africa. The word Religion we have in East Africa now mostly comes from the Arabic word *el dini* which means "a way of life." This leads us to considering further that religion in East Africa and Africa as a whole means life. It is a life-lived reality. This reality is lived and experienced, and is a by-product of people's perception of their nature, environment, human role, destiny and universe. All these make the seed of the ground of their understanding to take place. To understand the role is to admit the presence of the Master Creator.

An Africanist is a being that has great interest, respect and love for African life experience, and these aspects might be through birth, choice or both. In this experience an Africanist is not an observer or conceived clearly that the African worldview comes from the fact that no body can enter the religious participation without the Master creator. The Master Creator is the Maker of the World and nobody is an island. We live in communities and everyone is a participator of the communal practices.

In this understanding, the Creator is known as the Chief Educator of all creatures. The knowledge of the Master Creator is based on the assumptions underlying this understanding. Three of these assumptions are the following:

1. Religion inside and outside is based on philosophical and theological belief in Revelation. From this point

Elements of African Traditional Religion

of revelation Africans came to know God and how to worship this God.

2. The belief that religion is an absolute bond of the creator is what shapes the African life in relation to this Creator. There is not something in African life outside the relationship with the Creator. This is the main reason we say that African religion is the totality of life in relation to the Creator. And in this bond we understand that to talk of creation is to talk about God because God is the creator. This means that one cannot separate creation and the creator.

3. There is an aspect of religion and politics that are also inseparable. Politics is linked to the divine and religion is linked to politics. Politics is about people's lives and so is religion. This is the reason why in other countries Kings act as political and religious leaders; these two aspects cannot be separated because both are concerned with people's lives.

REVIEW QUESTIONS

1. Why should people, both Africans and non-Africans, study African Traditional Religion in this twenty-first century?

2. What does it mean to say that 'life' and 'religion' are inseparable in African context?

3. Why do you think comparative religionists excluded African Traditional Religion from being one among the Major World Religions? Discuss your reasons.

4. What is 'Religious concubinage'? Discuss the relationship between religious concubinage' and 'religious syncretism.'

Introduction

5. What does it mean to say that African Traditional Religion is not a 'bookish' religion?
6. With concrete reasons, state what is religion and what is not? Discuss the four (4) preliminary understanding of religion as described in this chapter.
7. What is the difference between the old and modern views on African Traditional Religion?

2

Beliefs, Rituals, and Symbols

INTRODUCTION

AFTER DESCRIBING BRIEFLY ABOUT religion and its link with people's lives in relation to the Creator, we now turn to looking at the way religion can be expressed in human practices. We look more closely at human beliefs, rituals and symbols in the practice of religion. As any other religion, a proper study of African Traditional Religion can be done in the light of people's beliefs, rituals and symbols as religious practices that manifest the existence of religion.

As we have just discussed in the previous paragraphs, the question to whether African Traditional Religion is a religion or not has received negative responses from theologians and lay people alike. These respondents mostly claim that African Traditional Religion is local. But, what makes a religion? Religion is composed of the following major aspects:

(i) Belief in the Supreme Being (God);

(ii) Practices of Worshipping the Supreme Being (God)

(iii) Naming and expressing the Supreme Being

BELIEFS

Does African Traditional Religion lack the above-mentioned aspects of religion? Taking Africa as a whole, there are five characteristics of beliefs that go with African Traditional Religion. These characteristics are the following:

(i) Belief in God

(ii) Belief in Divinities

(iii) Belief in Ancestors

(iv) Belief in Spirits

(v) The practice of medicine and magic

All the listed beliefs are life-lived practices of African Traditional Religion. Whatever might be said regarding the authenticity of these beliefs, the fact lies in those people who, through the experience of their beliefs, have come to realize their religion. In fact, it is not what we think about religion and its beliefs which is important; but, what is important is that which religion says or expresses itself in our experiences of it.

RITUALS AS SYMBOLS

In Africa, symbols are usually connected to *symbolic actions* known as *rituals*. Everywhere in Africa, human beings have a fundamental need to dramatize or celebrate their experiences or expectations through symbolic actions.

Elements of African Traditional Religion

Whichever view is taken, in Africa, rituals are highly important in dramatizing lived reality. This is because rituals are key to the understanding of the essential constitutions of human societies. Rituals stand as a bridge between verbal symbol and people's daily activities. Rituals are symbolic on the one hand, but they are a high point in human activity on the other. Through rituals an African person is able to make his/her experience clearer as he/she dramatizes and humanizes them to provide real meaning to the actions done. This means that rituals provide or put African people into reality and help them to restore or understand order in society. In this way, rituals help individuals to accept the claims of the society in a new state. Individuals can explain the conflicts and tensions and resolve them through the rituals performed. Therefore, as Mbiti clearly puts it: a ritual is a "means of communicating something of religious significance, through word, symbol and action."[1]

What we can emphasize here is that a ritual is a system of *ends* and *means* to an end. A ritual leads an individual to the ultimate goal. However, some rituals are merely expressive. They merely provide expression to human feeling or expectations. They say something about events but do not do something about them. Other rituals are instrumental. These ones tend not only expressing, but also trying to influence events to happen or prevent them from happening. Some people may be prevented from planting until the ritual has been fulfilled: this is an instrumental ritual. Examples of actions that were accompanied by instrumental rituals include the Mau Mau and the Maji Maji wars in Kenya and Tanzania respectively. Therefore, as already stated, the ritual becomes instrumental when it leads or prevents something to happen.

---

1. Mbiti, *Introduction to African Religion*, Second Edition, 131.

Beliefs, Rituals, and Symbols

One ritual which is popular in Africa is that of *initiation*. The word initiation comes from Latin *initare*, that means to begin, or beginning. Initiation means 'enter upon, or set going.' Most initiation rites are mysterious and are fully known to the initiates. The initiation ritual integrates, incorporates and involves the initiates into the mystery of the ritual. In this case, people who have undergone the initiation ritual are considered to be reborn and acquire a new status in the society.

There are three types of initiations that can be clearly known in African Traditional Religion: Puberty rights, Spirit initiation, and initiation to a mystical vocation. The cutting of bodies for example, during circumcision is a symbolic incorporation of young people into adulthood.[2] Marriage ceremonies, etc., are rituals that provide new statuses to those who instrumentally practice them. This is due to the fact that marriage in Africa is not just a mere coming together of two partners; it is more than that. Marriage, as an initiation ritual, is an essential cultic event centered on procreation. This means that the value of the man and woman in the family is not centered on the amount of wealth they possess, but on the number of mouths they are responsible to feed. This means that their value centers on their contribution on perpetuating and enhancing life on earth. Hence, for the African, without marriage there is no true human value, and marriage without children is totally incomplete.[3]

---

2. There are several countries that have adapted the circumcision ritual in the world and practice it more commonly. Some of such countries include the following: Egypt, Ethiopia, Somalia, Cameroon, South Africa, Zambia, Nigeria, Peru, Brazil, and the various Islamic countries of the Middle East, India and West Asia. Moreover, this ritual becomes common even in the Western world, cf. Sundermeier, *The Individual and the Community*, 59–69.

3. See Mbiti, *Introduction to African Religion*, Second Edition, 104–6.

Elements of African Traditional Religion

More generally we can say that a ritual instrumentally performed symbolizes rebirth from an old status. Baptism in Christianity symbolizes being born again and the death of the old status. Marriage in African traditional culture symbolizes true manhood and womanhood. Hence, in African worldview, the religious ritual sphere is a sphere per excellence, without any doubt, because through that ritual the world as lived and the world as imagined become fused together and transformed into one reality.

Theologian Peter Fue writes thus in regard to rituals as rites of passage: "Africans used to practice ritual separation under renowned professionals. A young person did not become a full member of the community unless he had undergone the ritual training, called *jando* and *unyago*, which prepared him for guardianship of society, parenthood and leadership. The *jando* and *unyago* was a seminar that prepared young people for married life and service to society."[4] This statement indicates that African societies cannot escape rituals as rights of passage to identify a particular person into a particular status in that society. The statement also purports that initiations are not mere rituals; they are also symbolic representations of the lived reality within the communities practicing the rituals.

Rituals, such as initiation rites are also performed for educational purposes and enhancement of unity and solidarity among young generations. Young men and women receive instructions on how to live as grown up people in solidarity to one another. Lema spells out more clearly when he writes: "A significant purpose of initiation was to unite all the initiates together into a strong brotherhood. The ties forged months of shared experience, hardships and teaching would remain steadfast in the fact of all the vicissitudes of adult life. Dances and songs in which all

4. Fue, "The Sermon on the Mount," 132.

Beliefs, Rituals, and Symbols

participated helped to intensify these emotional and social bonds. The food which the boys' families sent every day to the initiation camp was served by the teachers in a manner that emphasized their dependence on one another."[5] This means that rituals consolidated the identity of the society and strengthened the sense of ones belonging to that society through encouraging cohesion among members.

Spirit initiation occurs in the spirit cult. The initiate becomes possessed by the spirit and that spirit works though that individual. The possessed individual becomes a tool of the spirit and the spirit transfers its personality into the initiate. The initiate lives as a new person living in close associate with the spirit and his/her safety is protected from bad spells from his or her surroundings.

The *initiation to a mystical vocation* occurs when a ritual is performed to install a person to perform mystical duties. For example, a person can be initiated to be a medicine man or woman. In Christianity, the ordination of priests and pastors is a ritual to initiate people to new religious vocations. In this case, the initiation ritual becomes an experience of the initiate into a new position or mystical function where he/she has been initiated.

Through rituals human beings also transcend themselves and communicate directly with the divine. The experience of salvation becomes a present reality and not a future event. In short, almost every African ritual is a salvation event in which human experience is *recreated* and *renewed* in the all important rituals present. In so doing, the African recreates the concept of salvation.

Generally, rituals as symbols of African reality of life-lived experience are celebrated by experts. These experts are called ritual experts or specialists. These experts include the following: Priests, (ii) Diviners (iii) Prophets and (iv) Kings

5. Lema, "The Impact of Christianity," 70.

Elements of African Traditional Religion

or Chiefs. All these experts are the servants of the community. Their role is to mediate the community members through rituals. This means that African rituals have the sacred to specific religions and social functions; and this is clearly recognized by participants of the ritual performed.

In the time of colonial oppression in Africa and the rapid social political and cultural change, rituals and symbols enforced the creation of new social and political movements. As mentioned earlier, examples of these rituals and movements include *Maji Maji* wars in Tanzania the *Uhuru* Torch in Tanzania and *Mau Mau* in Kenya. These movements and wars have a ritual philosophy rather than being mere symbols. Hence, these movements and wars signify that ritual usage is very important in the understanding of African Religion and Philosophy.

SYMBOLS

We discussed symbolism in relation to rituals in the previous section. Let us now turn to looking at the concept of symbolism into a more detail. The word "symbol" comes from the Greek word '*symbalen*' (an aorist middle of *symballo*) which means "to recognize a guest, or to help or assist a guest." When a guest comes he/she is provided an invitation card or a ring or a staff. All these aspects play the role of making the guest feel at home. They are symbolic representation of something more than the invitation just done by the host.

The notion of symbolism is the base of all African oral communications and literature. A symbol is one of categories of signs with a multiple meanings, evoking emotions to those who see it leading them to action. For example, the Cross has many potential meanings and evokes emotions to people according to the meaning they decide to attach

Beliefs, Rituals, and Symbols

to it and leads them to actions. For Christians, the Cross mostly leads them to faith in Jesus Christ, because for them it is a symbol of Christ's suffering, trials and innocent death. The Crescent has many meanings; but, it is a symbol for the Muslims and their religion. However, these symbols are understood and have value only to the context and people where they are used.

Moreover, E.P. Sanders in his book *The Historical Figures of Jesus* states more clearly about the prophetic signs that had symbolic significance to people of the Old Testament when he says:

> Isaiah walked naked and with barefoot for three years as a sign of protest against Egypt and Ethiopia (cf. Isa. 20: 3). God commanded Jeremiah to break a pot and proclaim that the Temple would be destroyed (cf. Jer. 19: 1–3). Jeremiah also wore a yoke as a sign that Judah should submit to Babylon (cf. Chapters 27-8). Ezekiel performed much more complicated actions, which required a good deal of explanations, such as lying for long period of time first on one side and then on the other (cf. Ezek. chs.4–5; 12. 1–16; 24:15–24). These actions convey deep symbolic meanings, namely: wearing a yoke symbolizes submission; breaking a pot symbolizes destruction; and going naked and barefoot symbolizes protest.[6]

In a general sense, there is a difference between a sign and a symbol that needs our attention. A sign is anything that suggests something else. The word 'sign' originates from the Latin word '*signum*' that means 'token, mark, symptom, or warning.' A sign enables a person to foresee, guess, know or determine what is going to be. For example, the changing of water to wine done by Jesus helps to determine the

6. Sanders, *The Historical Figure*, 253.

presence of the Kingdom of God in the midst of people. It also helps to foresee or know who Jesus is.

There are two categories of signs. The two categories of signs are the following:

1. **Natural Signs:** These are images which suggest something else, e.g., an idea. Natural signs are signals which provide reflections to people, e.g., a tree, a bird, a snake, a cloud, etc.

2. **Conventional or Artificial Signs**: These are images made into signs by a human being himself or herself. These are called "man-made conventional signs. The best example of conventional signs is language. In language there is a sound image which is attached to an idea by convention. Different languages use different sounds or images to convey the same idea.

Contrary from signs, symbols are not usually explained, they speak by themselves through their existential contexts. The symbol offers a sense in itself. In most cases, a symbol explains, stands for, reveals, indicates, or helps to make the other reality more known to those who experience it. Revealing the secret of initiation ritual causes a severe punishment to the one who reveals it. Symbolic thinking is not pure reasoning because human beings are not fully in control of symbols. One cannot create a symbol as he/she can create a sign. For this reason, symbolic thinking has been called "committed thought" or "semi-incarnate thought" for example: In Christianity a candle signifies light against darkness. Moreover, Easter–night signifies resurrection.

Symbols are not allegorical because allegorical speaking speaks of something else, but symbols are tautological, i.e., they speak about the same thing they represent. The explanation of the symbol is provided by the context in which

Beliefs, Rituals, and Symbols

the symbol exists, for example; the cross in the church will express itself in the Christian religion; and the Crescent in Islam will express itself in the Islamic religion

A symbol is not a myth. A myth is often treated as if it was opposed to history, but the aim of history is to establish facts by evidence. The aim of myth is to teach the truth; but they can refuse to admit the fact provided by a symbol. People can also refuse to know symbols, especially as translated with ideas. In fact, what people can refuse to accept is the idea brought about by the symbol, not the symbol itself. This is because symbols can bring many ideas and meanings depending sorely on the way people interpret them.

Symbols can help people understand the more complex ideas such as those relating to religion. The only and most adequate way to speak about God is through symbols. It is through symbols that human beings can understand their relationship with God. In this way, Scripture and theology employ symbols to speak about God. In the Christian Scriptures, both the New and the Old Testaments, there are a lot of symbols which lead to the formulation of theology.

In Africa, human beings (people) experience God through symbolic perception not through reasoning alone. Reasoning may strengthen belief, but it is not the foundation of their beliefs. The power of God is discerned as Africans observe the symbols around them whose meanings make them appreciate wonders of the existence of God; and hence, they come into faith in this Supreme Being. Therefore, while other religions understand God through reasoning, African Traditional Religion understands God and the religion itself through symbolism. Through symbolism African Traditional Religion provides experience of the past and shares to its adherents the current experiences. Symbolism also enables people to classify and to humanize them into the society and the world they live in.

Elements of African Traditional Religion

The above statement means that symbolism is the point of contact with people and their mentality. The understanding of a particular society and its religion must start from symbolism. Symbols are models for behavior and conduct as well as of thinking capacity. Mythical symbols and ritual actions both function instrumentally. They are not in contradiction but go together. The major role they play is to try to shape the world in conformity with this reality. In doing that, some symbols are symbols which express the community past; or they highlight the structure and rites in the past for the benefit of the society.

It is very important to emphasize symbolism in the social cultural context where Africans live their lives. Understanding the symbolism in ethnic groups, in forests, grassland zones, and people who keep cattle will lead to the understanding of their general life. Symbolism has a key role in the African ethnic groups. In one sense, the African civilization and development is a civilization enhanced by symbolism because in Africa, the relationship between one person and another and the relation between one person and nature is enhanced by the use of symbols. In this interaction, symbolism is the key role towards the proper understanding of the real meaning of life. Through symbolism, Africans can understand the reality of invisible nature (e.g., God is invisible, but can be understood through symbols).

In Africa, the truly real is invisible and the visible is only appearance. This is why symbols are important to communicate the real which is invisible. And for Africans, symbolism is the unique way of maintaining and keeping their relationship with the universe. Through symbolism, they observe the universe as part of their life. The universe is visible and they can see it. What they try to do is to maintain their relationship with this Universe and God.[7]

7. Cf. Sundermeier, *The Individual and the Community*, 38–40.

Beliefs, Rituals, and Symbols

It important to emphasize here that symbols are specific and systematic. A particular symbol or symbols are understood and accessible *only* to insiders and not to outsiders. In this way symbols make a borderline between one community and another or one person and another. Symbols separate people into groups. The emergence of clans and societies in Africa is mostly due to identifications which are the results of the use of symbols. To deny Africans of their essential symbols is to deny their self-awareness. Ultimately, it is to take them away from their lived reality. This means that Africans live in a forest of symbols. Symbolism is a unique way of keeping their relationship with the Universe around them. Hence, we can summarize symbolism in African Traditional Religion by the words of Theo Sundermeier thus: "in Africa symbols link the past to the present; they link people to their environment, of which they are a part, and transform them. Symbols are mirrors of real life, mirrors of people in society and the cosmos. (. . .). [Therefore,] Symbols make Africans aware of themselves, and of the world in which they have a part."[8]

IMPORTANT VALUES

After discussing about the efficacy of symbols and symbolic use of them, we now turn to African values and their importance in African traditional Religion. Values are important aspects in any society because they are the source of cohesion among people. There is no society without values because they are cornerstones of conduct in any particularly recognized society. In the African society values are found in the African oral tradition and African oral literature. African oral literature is of very important source for discovering categories of thought or African values, or African

8. Sundermeier, *The individual and the Community*, 51–52.

Elements of African Traditional Religion

concepts of man, the concept of the world, of society, and of God. These categories are mostly found in *storytelling*. Storytelling is the chief way that social and moral values are imparted into African children by parents and grandparents in the African homes. Adult people take the priority in the art of storytelling to impart African values and ways of life. Adults are the initiators of stories that are rich in teachings about ways of life in particular African Societies. The major aim of storytelling in African societies is to pass the existing values of a particular society from one generation to the other.

The following are some of the literary forms of storytelling that are used to communicate African values from one generation to another.

1. **Didactic texts (Proverbs)**—These are statements about life. They are used to teach people. They remain purely at the level of observation and experience. An example of a proverb in an African context is this: "If a child cries for a razor, just offer it to him/her" or "Your neighbor's child is yours." These are some of the proverbs which teach about the societal and the value of inter-people's relations.

2. **Rituals**—We have already discussed this aspect in a more detail. However, due to its importance in African Traditional Religion as source of transmitting values, it is important that we remind ourselves once more here. Mbiti defines ritual to be "a set form of carrying out a religious action or ceremony. It is a means of communicating something of religious significance."[9] Prayers, invocations, oaths, curses and blessings, and magical spells are some of the major vehicles of African values communicated from one

---

9. Mbiti, *Introduction to African Religion*, Second Edition, 131.

Beliefs, Rituals, and Symbols

generation to another. In her article "Ritual Healing and Redefinition of Individual Personality in African Instituted Churches in Kenya," Philomena N. Mwaura identifies several types of rituals with different forms and contents: "technological rituals (carried out to control non-human nature), protective rites (to avert misfortune), therapy rites and rites injurious ends (like witchcraft and sorcery), identity rituals (directed to the control of the social group values e.g., rites of passage), social intensification rites to renew group solidarity (e.g., Sunday services), salvation rituals (aimed at enabling individuals to deal with personal difficulties), and revitalistic rituals (designed to cure society difficulties)."[10] All these types of rituals are good vehicles of transmitting African values from one generation to another.

3. **Riddles**—These are partly for instruction and partly for funny; and they also provide a hidden reality embodied within them. Examples of riddles more common in East African countries are the following presented in Swahili, Bena, and English:

 (a) *Nyumba yangu haina mlango—yai* (My house has got no door- an egg)

 (b) *Anayo macho lakini haoni—popo* (He has eyes but he does not see—bat)

 (c) *Anaona lakini yeye haonekani—Mungu* (He sees but he is not seen—God)

 (d) *Haonekani lakini yupo kila mahali—Mungu* (He is not seen, but is everywhere—God)

---

10. Mwaura, "Ritual Healing," 71.

(e) *Hamuogopi mfalme wala mtwana—njaa* (He is not afraid of a King or Subordinate—hunger/death/problems)[11]

(f) *Ihimtinava—ihisuhulunu (Bena). Kiungo usichoweza kulamba—kiwiko* (The organ near you which you cannot touch with your tongue—an elbow).

(g) *Umvengi umkova na vana—itulo. Mti wa matunda ambao hata mototo mchanga huweza kuchuma matunda yake—Usingizi* (A fruit tree whose fruits can be picked even by a small baby—falling asleep)

As one can note above, riddles are important instruments to impart to people the hidden reality much more simply in the course of funny. As people/children laugh, have funny, and try to search for an answer, they grasp what the riddle tells about the existing situation in their own lives.

4. **Etiological stories**—These stories tell us about the way things came to be as they are now, e.g., why hares have short tails, why a certain practice like circumcision came into being. Through stories such as these, good home morals are imparted to people who listen at them. These stories are just stories, but they are made real by using certain characteristics (values) embodied in them.

5. **Folktales**—Folktales may be difficult to differentiate from the rest but, in fact these stories are the ones that are told for their own sake. The main object is the story itself. This means that when telling this type of story, the credit is offered to the story itself.

---

11. Mbwilo, *Funzo la Kiswahili* (2011).

Beliefs, Rituals, and Symbols

Characteristically, these stories are short and clear, but with a heavy message in them.

6. **Myths**—"Myths are [symbolic] tales or traditions that seek to explain the place of man in the universe, the nature of society, the relationship between the individual and the world that he perceives, and the meaning of occurrences in nature."[12] Most African stories imply symbols and they are called myths. The myth itself is not important, but what is taught in that myth is what is important in the life of a particular society. For example, the myth of creation in Genesis, the myth of creation according to Mesopotamia, etc., are just myths. But what they try to teach the society is what matters greatly to the life of the society. Myths are important as they go together with the societal concepts of life. There are several myths in African Traditional Religion, e.g., marriage myths, creation, salvation myths, etc. (e.g., Genesis 1–11 is a myth).

Healey and Sybertz narrates one Sukuma creation myth of a cleaver young man (Masala Kulangwa) as it appears in the following paragraphs:

> Once upon a time, the monster Shing'weng'we swallowed the domestic animals together with all the people in the world except for one pregnant woman who hid in a pile of chaff. Later this woman gave birth to a boy named Masala Kulangwa. When he grew up he asked: 'Mother, why are there only the two of us? Where are the other people?' She answered: 'my dear one, everyone else was swallowed by the monster Shing'weng'we. We are the only ones left.
>
> From that day on, the clever young man started looking for the monster. One day he killed a

---

12. *The Illustrated Book*, 62.

grasshopper and arrived home singing: 'Mother, Mother, I have killed Shing'weng'we up in the hills. Rejoice and shout for joy.' But his Mother answered: 'My dear one, this is only a grasshopper, not the monster. Let's roast and eat it.'

Another day he killed a bird and arrived home singing: 'Mother, Mother, I have killed Shing'weng'we up in the hills. Rejoice and shout for joy.' But his mother answered: 'My dear one, this is only a bird, not the monster. Let's roast it and eat it.'

Another day, he killed a small gazelle and arrived home singing: 'Mother, Mother, I have killed Shing'weng'we up in the hills. Rejoice and shout for joy.' But his Mother answered: 'My dear one, this is only an antelope, not the monster, let's roast and eat it'.

When Masala Kulangwa grew to manhood, he told his mother that he wanted to go and look for the monster. At first she did not want him to go, but finally she agreed. Then he went out into the forest to look for the monster. Masala Kulangwa shouted, 'Hey, you, Shing'weng'we.' The monster answered, 'It's me', in a voice so loud that the earth shook. The clever young man was terrified, but he gritted his teeth and did not turn back.

Finally Masala Kulangwa found Shing'weng'we, overcame him, killed him and cut open the monster's back. Out came his father along with his relatives and all the other people. By bad luck, when he cut open the monster's back, Masala Kulangwa severed the ear of an old woman with his knife. This woman became very angry and insulted the young man. She tried to bewitch him and kill him. But Masala Kulangwa was guarded by his many friends, and she failed to harm him. Afterwards he found medicine

Beliefs, Rituals, and Symbols

and healed the old woman. Then all the people declared the clever young man chief and raised him up in the Chief's chair. Masala Kulangwa became the chief of the whole world, and his mother became the Queen mother.[13]

As I have noted above, the story and its characters are not enough, but what the story communicates is what is important. However, what is communicated in a mythical story is subject to interpretation and the meaning resides to the interpreter.

7. **Heroic recitations and Praise Poems (Swahili: Majigambo)**—These are statements that provide sentiment to an individual about a certain event. An individual stands before other people and speaks about his or her ability over others about something.

8. **Occassional poetry or songs**—These include song or poem of hunting, of harvesting, of circumcision, etc. These are not general, but are directed to particular events.

9. **Historical narratives**—These are straightforward accounts of the resent past's events, perhaps remembered by two or three generations. These provide interpretation, but not necessarily the historical fact of the narrative. The facts are there but not clearly presented. This means that in most African stories, the important thing is the *event* which that story presents not the *fact* of the story. This is because the event will enable people to discern the fact, according to the context of the listeners.

---

13. Healey & Sybertz, *Towards an African Narrative Theology*, 64—65.

Elements of African Traditional Religion

HEALING AND MEDICAL PRACTICES

One of the most important practices in most religions is the way its adherents can receive healing when they are faced by illnesses and suffering. Stinton clarifies this statement more clearly when she writes: "Religious figures commonly gain renown as healers, and sometimes the very salvation offered in particular religions is expressed in terms of diagnosis and cure: for example, in Buddha's Four Noble Truths, in the Hebrew Bible, the Qur'an, the Zoroastrian scriptures, and in the close relationship between and liberation in Taoism."[14]

In Christianity, Jesus as its foundering figure is considered as healer, the wonder worker who went throughout Galilee healing all kinds of infirmities to all those that were sick (Matthew 4: 23–25).[15] As the founder of the Christian religion, he seems to care people's wholeness by removing their sufferings that inflict them in one way or another. Hence, people find the meaning of religion when it interacts with them in their problems that make them discomfort physically, spiritually, and mentally.

However, the notion of Jesus as healer in the African context creates a great challenge in the midst of the existing suffering masses. Cece Kolie in his article "Jesus as Healer" points out clearly the dimension of this challenge within the African context when he writes: "To proclaim Jesus as the Great Healer calls for a great deal of explaining to the millions who starve in Sahel, to victims of injustice and corruption, and to the polyparasitic afflicted of the tropical and equatorial forests."[16] Kolie's statement above is more touching as one turns to the current real situation of the re-

14. Stinton, "Jesus as Healer," 13.

15. See also Ibid, 17.

16. Kolie,"Jesus as Healer," 128, cf. Mligo, *Jesus and the Stigmatized*, 366–71.

Beliefs, Rituals, and Symbols

surgence of incurable diseases and illnesses and their effects to people's lives. The Jesus who went throughout Galilee healing people's infirmities is put into question in regard to his present role in this confusing situation.

African Traditional Religion, as other world religions, is not a religion that has abandoned healing practices. Healing and wholeness is one of the sole concerns of this religion. In my recent book *The Pride of African Traditional Medicine*, I argue that God's healing ministry cannot be localized only to what we call 'biomedicine,' and neither can we confine God's dealing with humanity to only one religion. If African Traditional Religion is a religion through which God's dealing with humanity is realized, then healing is among such dealings that God works in various ways to maintain wholeness among African people. This means that God, the Healer, manifests the healing power in all religions including African Traditional Religion.

In African Traditional Religion, the healing practice is done through various agents: traditional medicine men and women, diviners and seers who act as laboratory technicians to diagnose the suffering and the source of this suffering, and ritual healers who perform healing through the administration of the required ritual as prescribed by the diviners. The healing is done by the use of herbal products that are mainly "derived from roots, barks, leaves and fruits from trees and plants. Other elements including bones, excreta, oils, skin, fur, feathers, fishes, animal products and other ingredients suitable for yielding medicinal extracts (. . .)."[17] Therefore, by the use of the mentioned healing materials and the approach to healing the whole person in the community (physically, mentally and spiritually), including the healing of relationships between people and their departed relatives and the natural environment surround-

17. Chepkwony, "Religion and Politics," 39.

ing people, traditional healers are regarded as 'community workers' who serve the purposes of their communities in various health matters.[18]

CONCLUSION

This chapter was concerned mainly about the description of the faith and practice of the adherents of African Traditional Religion. Three major aspects have been of great concern: major beliefs, ritual practices, and symbolic actions in African Traditional Religion. The belief in the existence of a Supreme Being and the hierarchy of divinities ancestors and the living dead are the core of all traditions within African despite their disparity in their worship practices. The belief and pride of African medical practices are as important as the people themselves. In this case, this chapter demonstrates that African Traditional Religion, as other religions in the world, involves people's faith in a certain Supreme Being and hierarchy of divine beings.

Through the Nyumbanitu traditional worship shrine, discussed in chapter four below, also demonstrates that the practice of African Traditional Religion is centered upon rituals that identify the individual within the community. Such rituals are symbolic actions that are mainly embedded within the culture of the individual. The main concern of rituals is to make a person traverse from one reality to another in his or her life. A person passes from childhood to youth stage or from youth stage to adulthood through the practice of a ritual, a symbolic action. Therefore, it becomes difficult to distinguish between life-lived symbolic actions and the religious life of the African because the two are closely intertwined.

18. Khamalwa, "Religion, Traditional Healers and the AIDS Pandemic," 91–92.

Beliefs, Rituals, and Symbols

Moreover, the chapter has highlighted the core values that bind the community members together. African Traditional Religious values are many and depend sorely on context and locality; but, the mentioned ones are important in almost all African cultures. The use of didactic texts, rituals, etiological stories, folktales, myths, heroic recitations and historical narratives in the interaction of people's daily lives is important in the communication of African people's cultural and religious lives.

Healing and medical practices are also part of African people's Religious lives. The practices of African Traditional healers are of vital importance to enhance life and diminish death among African people. This medical practice is religious in the sense that the essence of such healers to provide healing is the Supreme Being that works through them. Hence, the healing practices and the restoration of life among adherents is one of the important aspects in almost every religion.

REVIEW QUESTIONS

1. What do Africans believe in their African Traditional Religion? Why do you think they believe in that?

2. A ritual is a symbolic expression of what people believe and practice in a particular religion. Discuss this statement with special reference to African Traditional Religion.

3. What is a symbol and how does it differ from a sign, a myth, and an allegory? With the help of a traditional worship shrine found in your respective area, discuss the major religious symbols used by practitioners of African Traditional Religion and their importance in the life of Africans and their religion.

Elements of African Traditional Religion

4. Mention and discuss the major values of African Traditional Religion.
5. The question of healing and medical practice needs to be stipulated clearly in any relgion. Do you agree or disagree with this statement? Discuss it with special reference to African Traditional Religion.

3

The Concept of God

INTRODUCTION

IN THE PREVIOUS CHAPTER we concentrated much on the beliefs, rituals, symbols and values of African Traditional Religion. We discussed the importance of symbolism in the understanding of life among people in African societies. We also discussed the importance of values in holding the cohesion of social life and practice, and the ways through which such values are transferred from one generation to the other. In this case, the previous chapter clarified the ways in which African Traditional Religion is practiced and what aspects perpetuate it all along people's lives.

This chapter focuses on discussing the focal point of African Traditional Religion: the concept of God. What is 'god?' Is god, god to all people? There are many definitions that can be proposed in regard to the concept of god. Theologian Per Frostin proposes the following working definition: "god is a religious concept. As we all know there is a tendency to compartmentalize life in our culture, defining

Elements of African Traditional Religion

religion as one compartment beside the compartments of politics, economics, culture, sports etc. 'God' is then defined as related to the compartment of religion. (. . .). 'A god is what your heart clings to.'"[1] Frostin further states thus in regard to the determinant of a true and false god: "If your god gives you a good conscience, you believe in the true God (. . .). But if you get bad conscience and loose your confidence and openness, you have a false god."[2] Whether Frostin's definition holds truth is still a matter of discussion. However, following the definition suggested above, questions which may be raised are the following:

(i) What is the nature and purpose of the concept of God in African Traditional Religion?

(ii) Is there such a thing as an appropriate concept of God in African Traditional Religion regardless of the cultural differences existing among African peoples?

(iii) Is the Christian God, God of Abraham, Jacob and Isaac, and the Father of Jesus Christ the same God portrayed in African Traditional Religion?

Some basic statements to consider in regard to the questions above are the following:

1. If the Christian God is the same as that of African Traditional Religion, and if Christians knew God as the creator, the Sustainer, etc., then did Christianity bring anything new to Africa?

2. If the Christian God and that of African Traditional Religion are two different Gods why, from the beginning of Christianization in Africa, missionaries did not teach only about this God independently of the

1. Frostin, *Teologi som Befriar*, 110.
2. Ibid., 111.

The Concept of God

indigenous African concept of God? Did missionaries lack an appropriate way in which to explain the distinctly Christian God in an African context, or were they satisfied that the already deep-rooted indigenous concept of God was similar to the Christian concept of God, and hence was seen as a useful instrument in the Christianization process?

However, despite the two thought-provoking statements above, scholars have always agreed that Religion in Africa is a totality of life despite the many religious beliefs among African people. This is because despite their discrepancies in beliefs and practices, they have some characteristics in common: they have the same concept of God, they have a similar understanding of the spiritual nature of the world, the existence of spiritual powers within this world and the relationship Africans have with the world around them.[3] These mentioned aspects, and especially the same concept of God among various beliefs and practices in Africa, are unifying elements making African Traditional Religion to be one religion and not many religions.[4] It is this God of the Africans who is the primary cohesive power in every African cosmology, the power that unites the nature, history, spirits, ancestors, and even divinities which are the spiritual powers an African relates to.

This is not different from or opposite to the views of many other Christian theologians and missionaries, and some contemporary African scholars who describe monotheism to be at the heart of African Traditional Religion. More important, they argue that: traditional understanding of God share much in common with the Christian understanding of God. In fact, many African scholars continue

3. See Grebe & Fon, "African Traditional Religion," 95.

4. Chepkwony, "Religion and Politics," 35, cf. Mugambi, *Christianity and African Culture*, 140–141.

Elements of African Traditional Religion

to urge Christian scholars to re-assess their assumptions, about the uniqueness of the Christian God and to acknowledge that God's revelation is not limited to the Jews alone, but has been extended similarly to many other people as well.

John S. Mbiti once said that the missionaries who introduced the Gospel in Africa in the past 100 years did not bring God to our African continent; instead, God who was already present in the continent of Africa brought them there. The missionaries proclaimed Jesus Christ and His message of salvation as understood in Christian perspectives; but they used the names of God as were used by the indigenous Africans. For example the names Mulungu, Inguluvi, Katonda, Ngai, Modimo, etc., were used by missionaries to name God of Christianity. These names describe the only one God who was known by Africans in different names. Therefore the African names were not empty names. They are names of one and the same God, the creator of the whole world and the Father of the Lord Jesus Christ.

Africans in various societies have no doubt that everyone knows about God. In this understanding, therefore, Africans have many names for God depending on the ethnic group. And in fact, no single name is adequate in describing all attributes of God. Moreover, we need to make it clear that African's metaphor for God make them understand God as neither male nor female. This means that there is no one gender orientation is embraced for the one God understood by Africans and called in different names. In some parts of Africa God is known as she-God (feminine), others identify God as he-God (masculine), while others identify God in both feminine and masculine (e.g., the Ndebele and Shona people of Zimbabwe). The Nuba of Sudan understand God as the Great Mother and they use a feminine pronoun (she) to pronounce this God. This also applies to

The Concept of God

the Ovabo of Namibia and the Iraqw of Tanzania.[5] But the Hehe and Bena of Iringa and Njombe respectively, Mulungu and Inguluvi are masculine. God is conceived in these ethnic groups as being male.[6] However, the Swahili word *Mungu* which is used by the various ethnic groups to name their Supreme Beings, including *Nguluvi* of the Hehe and Bena, and *Looa* of the Iraqw is gender neutral.[7]

In this case, in African understanding of God there is much less sexist than in other many world religions, e.g., Christianity, Islam, Judaism, etc. When we say that African Traditional Religion is not sexist, we mean that though God is known by different names, some feminine others masculine, their emphasis are not in the sexism of God but on the *attributes* of God according to the particular people (or society).

ATTRIBUTES OF GOD

The word "attribute" refers to what something become as it is. Attributes of God are what makes God in an African understanding. In Africa, God is provided titles or names called attributes which many Africans think as being the characters of God. But one common attribute is *God as the creator*. Other attributes include God as Provider of life, Provider of Rain, God as the Cause of seasons, Provider of sunshine, etc. These names are used to indicate the limitless

5. Mojola, "The Global Context," 62, 65.

6. Ibid., 63.

7. Ibid., 62–64, 67. Kiswahili is a Bantu related language which is spoken by the majority of people in the East and Central African ethnic groups. This means that all the ethnic groups using Kiswahili within this region use the name '*Mungu*' for their Supreme Being with regardless to whether that Supreme Being has a masculine or feminine traditional name as it is for *Looa* and *Mulungu*.

Elements of African Traditional Religion

power of God. Other attributes indicate that God knows everything is present everywhere, is almighty, etc. Theologian Aloo Mojola writes thus about the attributes of Looa, the God of the Iraqw in Mbulu Tanzania: "Looa (. . .) is believed to be loving and kind. She is the provider, the protector, the merciful, the giver of life. She is the creator, the giver of children and blessings. She is light. She is the sun. She watches over all. She is opposed to darkness. She is the one every Iraqw prays to for protection. She is the one dear to every Iraqw. She is the one on the lips of every Iraqw, Christian or non-Christian, at a time of danger."[8] We will discuss some of these attributes below:[9]

God is unknowable

This attribute according to African understanding, indicates that God is beyond human comprehension. God cannot be fully comprehended and articulated according to the way the human being has comprehended. But, however, when one sees the world and its harmony, he/she is indebted to discern this God. In chapter four below, it will be illustrated that Shalula, the Creator of the Bena, is unknowable, the first and the last being beyond human comprehension.

The Supreme Being of the Africans is Omnipotent

In traditional African understanding of the Supreme Being, the Supreme Being is *Imminent* and Transcendent at

---

8. Mojola, "The Global Context and Its Consequences," 65.

9. For more descriptions about the attributes of God in African Traditional Religion see Mbiti, *Introduction to African Religion*, Second Edition, 49–59; cf. Sundermeier, *The Individual and the Community*, 159.

The Concept of God

the same time. The Supreme Being becomes, visible when exercising the power over creatures, the power to regulate nature. Let us take God of Wabena of Njombe as an example to illustrate this point. The Supreme Being of Wabena is called "*Nguluvi*" even though the synonym "*Mulungu*" is used for the same purpose. However, in the current understanding of the Wabena, the later has to stand for the Christian day of worship (Sunday). To the Wabena, *Mulungu* is the last day of the week. The worship of "*Nguluvi*" to the Wabena is not more vivid, especially in the current world, but people still recognize the existence of the spirits and the ancestors through whom the living are connected to those in the life after death, and hence are connected to Nguluvi their creator. Among the Bena in Njombe, *Nguluvi* (God) is unquestionably powerful. *Nguluvi* has power over spirits and is able to control them. According to the Bena, *Nguluvi* is unknowable and unapproachable, but is experienced through the works of controlling harmony in the Bena society.[10]

The Supreme Being of the Africans is Omniscient

Africans believe in the limitedness of their minds and knowledge in regard to some issues surrounding their lives. When they consider about the Supreme Being, they see this Supreme Being as being unlimited, the one that knows everything beyond their own thinking and acting. The Supreme Being is the wise one who settles all matters and sees the whole inside and outside of human beings. Being an Omniscient, the Supreme Being among the Bena is considered to be the hearer and the watcher of everything thought and done by people in the society. In this case, among the

10. For more elaboration of the worship and beliefs of the Bena about God see chapter four below.

Elements of African Traditional Religion

Bena, the belief in the complete knowledge of *Nguluvi* is embraced. *Nguluvi* is believed by the Wabena as the one to whom nothing can be hidden.[11]

The Supreme Being of the Africans is Omnipresent

The traditional African belief holds that the Supreme Being is present everywhere. This means that the Supreme Being "is accessible to people through prayer and that he [she] cares for the well being of humanity by providing rain and all necessities of life."[12] However, Africans still admit that due to the limitedness of humanity, one cannot be and not be at the same time, and one cannot be present at more than one place at the same time. In virtue of their knowledge of the limitlessness of God, they believe that the Supreme Being is present everywhere at the same time. Jesse Mugambi and Nicodemus Kirima write thus: "When men or women are captured by an enemy during a war in a foreign land, the captives beseech their God to deliver them back home."[13] Mugambi and Kirima's statement above testify people's belief that God is present in all places where people are, and can deliver them from all dangers and harm. The Bena of Njombe and the Hehe of Iringa in Tanzania also believe on the Omnipresence of their Supreme Being (Nguluvi). They believe *Nguluvi* to be a spirit, and with this form *Nguluvi* is believed to be everywhere though one cannot see this God with his/her naked eyes.[14]

---

11. Cf. the description in chapter four below.

12. Chepkwony, "Forgiveness," 142. The Kalenjin ethnic group of Kenya believes in the omnipresence, accessibility, and providence of *Isis* their Supreme Being.

13. Mugambi & Kirima, *African Religious Heritage*, 126.

14. See chapter four below for more elaboration.

The Concept of God

However, this God is present through the power or life force that exists in all creatures. The God of the Africans cannot be disturbed because this God is holy. The divine presence of this God is manifested through the natural powers through which human beings approach God. Many scholars agree that the God of the Africans is omnipresent, put his manifestation is through the life force that is entrusted to all created beings. Grebe and Fon write that in order for an African to deal with his or her problems he/she has to use certain objects provided by the Supreme God in order to protect oneself or sacrifice to ancestors in order to appease them. In this case, the person has to use the means which God provided in order to protect oneself from or get rid of problems because every object or means that the person uses reflects the presence of the Creator by possessing the life force.[15]

The Supreme Being of the Africans is Everlasting

This attribute refers to the uncreatedness of the Supreme Being according to Africans. While all other creatures were created by the Supreme Being, No one created the Supreme Being. This means that the Supreme Being has neither beginning nor end. This is what actually means by everlasting.

The Supreme Being of the Africans is Spirit

The Supreme Being is invisible and intangible, but real. What is real is invisible and what is visible is just appearance. This is the great philosophy of African life. African Traditional Religion has no animism as claimed by some

15. Grebe & Fon, "African Traditional Religion," 95; cf. Mgeyekwa, "The Understanding of Salvation," (2011).

Christian scholars.[16] The concept of Animism was created by Europeans. However, from the point of view that God is spirit, God is not fashioned in wood materials, drawing or stones.

The Supreme Being of Africans is kind

Kindness goes together with provision. The Supreme Being is in the manner that when asked for something, it is provided abundantly. Even when not asked the Supreme Being provides and sustains people's lives. The Supreme Being provides food, rain, children, etc., to all kinds of people and in all kinds of situations.

The Supreme Being of the Africans is Holy

The holiness of the Supreme Being is viewed in relation to creatures created by this Supreme Being. Creatures are wrong doors naturally. The Supreme Being is separated from creatures because of being transcendent and inapproachable by human beings.[17]

The Supreme Being of the Africans is Unique

The Uniqueness of the Supreme Being is based on comparison with other creatures. The Supreme Being cannot be compared with anything that exists in whatever way.

---

16. See Furre, "The Brazilian 'Universal Church of the Kingdom of God,'" 41.

17. Nguluvi or Mulungu, the Supreme Being of the Bena shrine at Nyumbanitu, for example, is too holy to mention the name of this God. For more elaboration see the descriptions provided in chapter four below.

The Concept of God

All these attributes speak something about the work of the Supreme Being according to African Traditional Religion.

The attributes of the Supreme being mentioned above are strongly held by the worshippers at the Nyumbanitu traditional worship at Njombe Tanzania. The priests of Nyumbanitu shrine related that people that went at Nyumbanitu for worship believe in only one Supreme Being under the name of Nguluvi or Mulungu who is assisted by the ancestors, divinities and spirits in order to bring harmony to the life of worshippers. Hence, the worship at Nyumbanitu represents the reality of African understanding of God irrespective of their diverse ethnic belonging.

ON SEEKING THE EFFICACY OF AFRICAN TRADITIONAL RELIGIOUS WORSHIP

After discussing the various attributes of the Supreme Being according to African Traditional Religion, it is important to discuss briefly on the validity of African Traditional Religious worship itself. There are several questions that can enlighten us in discussing African Traditional Religious worship. Is African Traditional Religious worshiping really the worship of the Almighty God? How is this worship done and what are people's conceptions about this type of worship? We will now describe the way sacrifices are provided and prayers and invocations towards the Supreme Being are done according to African Traditional worship.

Sacrifices in African Traditional Worship

Sacrifices and offering mark the centre of African worship ritual. African sacrifices and offerings are not offered directly to God the Almighty; but they are offered to ancestors or spirits who are more powerful than human beings. These

Elements of African Traditional Religion

ancestors are believed by Africans as being their mediators between them and God.

When the need for sacrificing arises, there are special elders who are set apart for this purpose. Among the Wabena of Njombe (at Nyumbanitu worship shrine) these elders are called "*vatehedzi*"—the priests or mediators. The action of sacrificing is called "*hutehela*" or "*hutambiha*"—that is to sacrifice. The materials offered for sacrifice are among the food materials eaten by the Wabena people. However, in its strict sense only animals and cereal crops are used for sacrifices among the Wabena ethnic group.

In most African sacrifices, the places for sacrifices depend on the families or social groups and the occasion for which to sacrifice. The places are set apart and are regarded as sacred where no cultivation is allowed.

The daily libations among the Wabena are poured by the heads of the families. Usually the father or the first-born male of the family if the father has died. This activity of daily libation is done by other African tribes also apart from the Wabena of Njombe. Among the Kamba in Kenya, "The daily libation," according to J.M. Bahemuka, "are offered by the head of the family at the beginning of the meal."[18] The reason to why sacrifices should be offered is summarized by Mbiti as he writes:

> They are also acts and occasions of making and renewing contact with God and man, the spirits and man. When they are directed to the departed, they are a symbol of fellowship, recognition that the departed are still members of their human families and tokens of respect and remembrance of the departed.[19]

18. Bahemuka, *Our Religious Heritage*, 59.
19. Mbiti, *Concepts of God*, 179.

The Concept of God

Mbiti's statement above describes the link between God and thriving people, God and the departed, and the living and the departed. Mbiti emphasizes that the departed are still members of the families and still need respect and remembrance. Acts of sacrifices are acts of remembrance to the departed and at the same time acts of honour to God the almighty.

Prayers and Invocations in African Traditional Religious Worship

It is guaranteed that sacrifices and offerings must be accompanied by prayers. However, when only prayers are needed sacrifices are not necessary. African religious people pray short prayers but directed to the point. These prayers are directed either to the Supreme Being or to ancestral spirits as mediators.

Prayers and supplications are directed to God or Ancestral spirits when there is a need for God's favor upon people's crops, guidance of cattle, and safety from diseases and even victory from war.

Invocations are shorter prayers prayed by an individual. These are spontaneous responses to God, asking for God's intervention to certain unfavourable situations in our day to day lives. In actual fact, African prayers are based on or centered on a tribe or clan and their ancestral spirits. Every member of the tribe or clan prays though sometimes only leaders may be reciting words.

CONCLUSION

There has been a problem of some people to think that the African concept of God is Satanic and obscure. This is probably not the right way of looking at other religions. If one looks with a close eye, he/she can realize that, nowhere, in any religion whatsoever, where the concept of God is as clear as one may think it to be. The obscurity found in the mystery of the Trinity in Christianity, the obscurity of the Quranic dictation by God to Muhammad (*tanzil*) in Islam, and the obscurity of the concept of God in African Traditional religion, etc., all verify the same unknowable and unapproachable Supreme Being.

E. Bolaji Idowu provides a warning about the problem of looking at other people's religions negatively thus:

> Those who take one look at other people's religion and assert glibly that such people have no clear concept of God, or no concept of God at all, should first look within themselves and face honestly the question; how clear is the concept of God to me? How clear is the concept of God to my own people (. . .)?[20]

The above statement indicates that an endeavor to jeopardize other people's religions and their understanding of God is caused by the lack of clear understanding of their worldview. It has nothing to do with truth because the truth is upon those who experience and practice that religion.

It is plausible for people to appreciate the differences in the concepts of God among the different tribes and societies in Africa. Some believe in the masculine Supreme Being (e.g., the Bena) others believe in the feminine Supreme Being and everyone has a local name for God. But this has to do with the cultural backgrounds of the tribe and has nothing to do with the adulteration of the whole concept of God which the tribe has. Therefore, however conceived God remains and will remain real and Supreme Being in

20. Idowu, *African Traditional Religion*, 143.

The Concept of God

African Traditional Religion. Unless the African values are well understood and viewed, the true understanding of Christianity as a new religion in the African soil will greatly be hindered.

REVIEW QUESTIONS

1. What does it mean by 'god' according to Per Frostin? With concrete evidence, discuss Frostin's definition of god.
2. John S. Mbiti once said that missionaries did not bring God to Africa, but God brought them to Africa. Discuss the efficacy of Mbiti's statement in relation to African concept of God.
3. Discuss the major attributes of God according to African Traditional Religion. How are these attributes different from those of other world religions?
4. With special reference to a particular shrine from your own tribe or ethnic group, discuss the way in which the worship of God is done in African Traditional Religion.

4

The Bena Worship at Nyumbanitu Shrine

INTRODUCTION

AN ILLUSTRATION OF AFRICAN Traditional worship is found at Nyumbanitu shrine that still conducts services for the worship of *Mulungu* or *Nguluvi* until now. Nyumbanitu worship shrine is located at Mlevela village, Mdandu Ward, Imalinyi Division, Wanging'ombe District, Njombe Region in Tanzania.[1] It is about twenty five kilometers from Njombe town, the headquarters of Njombe Region and is surrounded by the Wattle Company forests. In this case, Nyumbanitu shrine is an important worship place that preserves the traditions of the Bena ethnic group.

---

1. The description presented in this chapter is based on the research visit to Nyumbanitu carried out by myself together with my two research assistants Innocent Pius Kibadu and Stanley Nicolaus Kambo on 30 May, 2013. We had a high time to learn from the great treasure of Bena traditions preserved at Nyumbanitu worship shrine. All photos for illustration placed in this chapter were taken by Stanley Kambo.

The Bena Worship at Nyumbanitu Shrine

Figure 1: The poster situated across the road to tell people about the Nyumbanitu Forest

The Worship of Mulungu or Nguluvi at Nyumbanitu is not only practiced by the Bena who are the residents of the area, but also by the nearby ethnic groups whose origin is Nyumbanitu. These ethnic groups include: the Kinga, the Wanji, the Sangu and the Hehe ethnic groups. The traditional worship service at Nyumbanitu is a cooperate worship whereby many people participate under the priest of the shrine. The worship service mainly depends on who wants to offer sacrifices and for what main purpose.

The Nyumbanitu shrine is divided into two parts: the Nyumbanitu forest, and the Nyumbanitu cave. However, these to places, through located almost one kilometer apart, are one and both are dwelling places of the Bena ancestral spirits. The worship service always commences at the Nyumbanitu forest and ends at the Nyumbanitu cave. Some of the services end only at the Forest depending on the weight of the problems of the worshippers. This chapter is therefore dedicated to describing the way worships and symbolisms are presented at the two places of Nyumbanitu Bena worship shrine: Nyumbanitu Forest and Nyumbanitu Cave.

THE NYUMBANITU FOREST

Nyumbanitu Forest is about three acres large and is full of natural vegetation. Most trees at this forest are medicinal; and can be used for healing of various human and animal diseases. The forest is decorated by mystic black chicken that dwell in the forest. These chicken mostly appear during the harvesting season and disappear after that season. Cutting of tree in this forest is not allowed because nobody is allowed to enter it without permission from the ancestors that dwell in it. In this case, the forest is full of natural grass and humus due to the decomposition of leaves that fell down from trees every year.

Entering the Shrine

Entering the Nyumbanitu shrine takes place through the Nyumbanitu Forest, the first part of the shrine. Before entering the Nyumbanitu shrine, worshippers and any other people entering the shrine take off their shoes, hats or veils because they approach a holy place. They approach the dwelling place of the ancestors full of divine magnificence. This means that the veneration of ancestors does not start after approaching the altar, but even before entering the Nyumbanitu shrine itself.

The Bena Worship at Nyumbanitu Shrine

Figure 2: The Entrance to the worship shrine
at Nyumbanitu Forest. Entering the shrine is by single file

Figure 3: Before approaching the Altar, shoes, veils
and hats must be taken out.

Elements of African Traditional Religion

The entrance door to the altar of the shrine is always closed and nobody is allowed to enter the shrine without permission from the responsible priests, and without a concrete worship or visit reason. Before entering the shrine, the priest knocks the door by picking a leaf from one of the trees at the entrance spitting out saliva on it while pronouncing special words to the ancestors of the shrine. The words are just for asking permission from the ancestors to allow people visit or worship. Hence, after these words are pronounced the priest together with other worshippers enter the shrine and approach the altar place.

Worship Process at the Altar

While at the altar, the priest puts on the black rob and kneels at the altar to commence the traditional worship. The worship continues by the priest pronouncing the words according to the needs of the worshippers: this may be fertility, rain, crops, success in war, etc. Every time the priest mentions something, it is accompanied by the name of the ancestor of the clan responsible for that issue.

Figure 4: The Altar and its decoration with liturgical symbols

The Bena Worship at Nyumbanitu Shrine

The words of the priest are pronounced after mixing the flour of finger millet and water pouring the mixture at a small hole near the big tree where the altar is located. This practice symbolizes the worshippers' offering of food and water to the ancestors in order to appease and let them hear their prayers and supplications. During the traditional worship at Nyumbanitu, various kinds of sacrifices are offered: animals like goats, cattle, sheep, and chicken all being black in color. Some worshippers provide money as sacrifices in order to receive blessings from God through ancestors. This practice indicates that worshippers at Nyumbanitu are aware of the existence of the Supreme Being who is approached through the ancestors of the shrine.

The Major Bena Ancestral Clans

Accoridng to the explanations of the priests, there are about eleven ancestral clans responsible for the Nyumbanitu worship shrine. These major clans are the following: the Shalula, Tevele, Mkilaugi, Mponda, Ng'anzagala, Malova, Mafyata, Ngiliviga, Kahemele, Mhimba, and Shalula. The priests also related that one of these ancestral spirits (Shalula) is the highest of all. Shalula is the one who created the world and all that is in it (*ye alwe ivinu vyonda ivilimunyi*). Shalula is unknown and unapproachable. Shalula is the attribute of Nguluvi, the God of the Bena. Therefore Shalula is considered to be the first and the last ancestor.

Brief Historical Background of Worship at Nyumbanitu

Historically, the worship that continues at Nyumbanitu now originates from the clan of Kahemele. Kahemele had three sons. When he became old, he decided to provide each of them a portion of inheritance. Kahemele put three things (a hoe, a spear, and a small winnowing mat [*ungo*]) before his sons and urged them to compete in picking each of them what he wanted. They were to run towards where Kahemele placed the things in competition way. Kahemele did not want to just provide them. He wanted each of them to pick what he wanted after reaching the place where they were placed. Kahemele provided the names of the sons according to what each one picked at the destination. The youngest son ran quickly and was the first to reach the destination. He picked a spear and was called Mkongwa because he was to be responsible for guarding other Benas in wars and misfortunes. Kahemele pronounced the words of installation to him: "*ukongage avayago wonda, uhomage amagoha pamwinga nawo*" (You have to guard all your fellow citizens, fight the wars with them). So, the Mkongwa sub-clan from Kahemele clan became the guardians for the Bena and the nearby tribes that worship at Nyumbanitu.

The Bena Worship at Nyumbanitu Shrine

Figure 5: A spear symbolizes the responsibility to fight war to protect other Bena people from enemies

The eldest son was the second to reach the destination. He picked a hoe and was made responsible for feeding and sustaining the livelihoods of all other people. He was called Fute. To this son, the words of installation were pronounced thus: "*futilage uhulima; lisage avayago wonda*" (work hard in your farming work; feed all your fellow citizens). Feeding and cultivating, according to the explanations of the priests, were not mere faming work. The words symbolized 'protection'. The hoe provided to Fute was itself a symbol of what the Bena call *Ngimo*, i.e., a traditional weapon for protection. Therefore, the Fute sub-clan was responsible in all matters concerning protection.

Elements of African Traditional Religion

Figure 6: A hoe symbolizes the responsibility to feed
and sustain other Bena people.

The second son was the last to reach the destination. He picked a winnowing mat (*ungo*). He was made responsible for worship issues and was called Kiswaga. The words of installation for him were the following: "*uswagage avanu wonda vikalage pa litambiho lya nyumbanitu*" (lead all people towards adhering to the worship at the Nyumbanitu shrine). Therefore, the winnowing mat was a symbol of worship and adoration of God through the provision of sacrifices to the ancestors.

The Bena Worship at Nyumbanitu Shrine

Figure 7: The small winnowing mat symbolizes the responsibility to conduct worship services and sacrifices for people's problems.

Types of Worship Services at Nyumbanitu Shrine

There are two major types of worship services conducted at Nyumbanitu worship shrine twice a year. The first worship is accompanied by prayers to Nguluvi to provide people with a conducive environment to succeed in their cultivations and livestock keeping. This is done between October and December which is the rainy seasons of most dwelling places of the Bena people. The second worship service is accompanied by thanksgiving to ancestors for making a fortune to people's endeavors. The worship is accompanied by celebrations and cheers whereby people rejoice their success in various life issues including harvest, prosperity in livestock keeping, and the birth of children. This worship is done between June and August which is the harvest season among most of the Bena areas. However, some occasional worship services are frequently conducted for people who approach the shrine due to their life problems. Therefore, Nyumbanitu is a place of refuge to those in trouble and a place whereby people communicate with Shalula (the Creator of all that exist) through prayers, supplications, and sacrifices to their ancestors.

THE NYUMBANITU CAVE

Most worship services are conducted at Nyumbanitu forest discussed above. If there is a big problem the priests conduct special services at Nyumbanitu cave. This means that there is a relationship between Nyumbanitu cave and Nyumbanitu forest. Both of them form what is known as Nyumbanitu worship shrine.

Figure 8: The entrance to the Nyumbanitu cave. In this figure, the author enters the cave.

Relationship between the Nyumbanitu Cave and the Nyumbanitu Forest

The cave has the entrance and exit doors. Once worshippers and visitors enter the cave, they do not go out through the entrance door. There is another door that is special for exit. Moreover, there is no need to knock the door to ancestors while entering the cave. The priests related that both worshippers and visitors have to knock the door only once at the Nyumbanitu forest and that will be enough. This means that the worship or visit always starts at the forest and is consummated at the cave. Therefore one cannot enter the cave or forest without knocking the door to the ancestors; and knocking is done only at the forest.

What is the relationship between Nyumbanitu forest and Nyumbanitu cave? According to the descriptions of the priests of the shrine, the cave was the sleeping place of mystic cattle of the shrine and the forest was the place where these mystic cattle stayed during the day. The priests of Nyumbanitu shrine were quite open that the mystic cattle moved from the cave to the forest every morning, a distance of about one kilometer apart, and returned back to the cave for sleeping every evening. The heavy mist surrounded the cattle and moved with them. Nobody saw the cattle themselves and their keepers. When those cattle passed by the houses of the people, such people just saw the heavy mist passing and heard the voices of the cattle bells and the voices of the keepers. This means that those cattle were not normal visible cattle, and the keepers were not normal visible keepers.

Elements of African Traditional Religion

Figure 9: The kraal where the mystic cattle slept at the cave during the night.

The Cave as a Manifestation of God's Natural Revelation

The Nyumbanitu cave is full of the wonders of God's creative power. It is a place where the faith of the Bena worshippers dwells. When the Bena talk about Shalula as being the creator of all that exists, they mostly refer to the wonders that Shalula has done at Nyumbanitu. The creation of the Nyumbanitu cave and the shapes of the rooms inside it evokes faith in the existence of Shalula (Nguluvi) who created all that exists. In my judgment, the worship and faith of the Bena is based on the natural revelation. According to the Bena, God reveals oneself through the wonders of the existing creation; and the Nyumbanitu cave is one such wonders of the creative power of God that evokes faith in the existence of this God.

The Bena Worship at Nyumbanitu Shrine

Figure 10: The wonders of the Nyumbanitu cave:
this is a sitting room where people stayed during war time
hiding from their enemies. The dark room at the left hand side
behind the priest is entrance door to the holy of holies room.

The Holy of Holies at the Cave

While at the cave the priests showed us one room that was very special. The priests told us that nobody was allowed to enter that room, including the priests themselves. As for the priests, they were allowed to enter it only if a special prayer for people's problems was to be done, and only for the permission from ancestors. However, they had to purify themselves before entering it. If they had misunderstandings or quarrels with their wives at homes, their relatives or neighbors, they were not allowed to enter such a room. If they had sexual intercourse out of their official marriages, they were also not allowed to enter the room. In this case, the room was a holy of holies set apart for special prayers ad could not be adulterated by any kind of dirty.

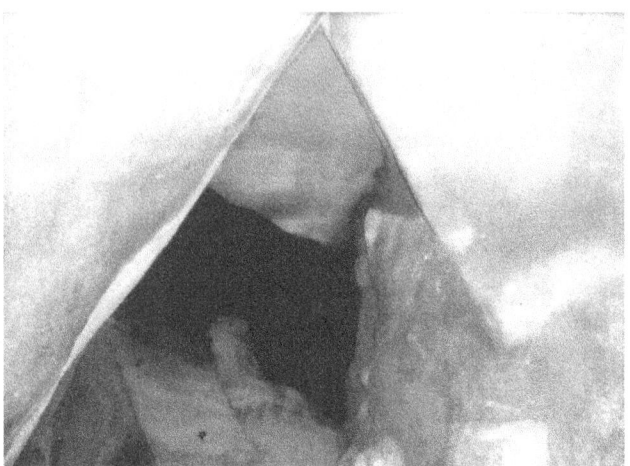

Figure 11: Entrance door to the Holy of Holies Room at Nyumbanitu Cave

Since this room at Nyumbanitu cave could be entered only by priests in order to pray for people's problems, it greatly resembles the Temple at Jerusalem during the Jewish time. According to the Jewish Religion, the priest entered the Holy of Holies only once per year in order to pray for people's sins. It is possible to make this comparison because, as it seems, only one God is working to direct worship and adoration to both Judaism and the worship of the Bena at Nyumbanitu!

SYMBOLISM AT NYUMBANITU SHRINE

Nyumbanitu shrine is a good illustration of the current use of symbols in traditional African worship activities. The symbolism at Nyumbanitu is found in the forest, caves, and the decorations of the altar.

The Forest and Its Caves

The forest surrounding the Nyumbanitu shrine has a special meaning. According to the explanations of the Priests of the shrine, the word "*Nyumbanitu*" has its origin from the interethnic or tribal wars, when the Bena ethnic group fought with its nearby ethnic groups, for example the Sangu and the Hehe ethnic groups. The Bena people believed that they could hide themselves within the forest without being viewed by their enemies; even though the Bena themselves viewed their enemies as they passed by them. The enemies could not view the Bena because the ancestors that dwell within the forest protected them by creating darkness to the enemies though they stood at an open space within the forest. In this case, the forest stood as a symbol of a 'protective house' whereby people could take refuge in the time of terror and misfortune.

Priests of the shrine also related that "Nyumbanitu" means "*darkness*." By "*darkness*" it means the dark situation inside the caves whereby people hid themselves during wars or misfortunes. The cave has 16 rooms and each is dark with a lot of bates inside. It is believed that if a person tries to enter the rooms of the cave without the priests he/she cannot find the door because that person will have no permission from the ancestors of the shrine. This means that a house is made dark by the ancestors in order for it to be a house for people to take refuge.

Priests also accounted for the symbolism of "Nyumbanitu" in terms of the various symbols that are used for worship purposes: a dark cloth, dark chicken, a dark goat, and a dark cow. These are the items that are used for sacrifices to God during worship at Nyumbanitu shrine. This means that "darkness" is a symbol of refuge, especially during the time of terror, and it characterizes the whole activity that is carried out at the shrine and all that is within it.

Elements of African Traditional Religion

Other Symbols at Nyumbanitu Warship Altar

The altar of Nyumbanitu worship shrine is decorated by symbols under one of the big trees of the forest. Some of such symbols include the following:

1. A spear symbolizes wars fought during interethnic conflicts between the Bena ethnic group and its nearby tribes. The clan of Kiswaga was the major proponent of war for protecting other Bena clans against enemies.

2. A hoe symbolizes agriculture, the major activity among the Bena and the nearby ethnic groups. The clan of Mkongwa was responsible for agricultural activities to feed other Bena clans.

3. The flour made from finger millet symbolizes the food of the ancestors, the elders that founded the Bena ethnic group. According to the priests the name 'Bena' comes from the hervest activity of finger millet which was the main crop of the Bena ancestors. They were known as "*vabenuledzi*" (harvesters of finger millet), hence their name *Vabena*.

4. A three-legged chair symbolizes the kingdom or priesthood. It indicates that the one that presides at the worship has to seat on a royal typical Bena chair. This chair is only for the priest that presides in the worship service.

5. A small pot symbolizes the preservation of old Bena traditions whereby the past ancestors used pots to keep milk.

6. A black rob with three marks of the cross behind, and at the hand sides just below the shoulder symbolizes how broad is the duty of priesthood to intercede for people's problems during worship.

The Bena Worship at Nyumbanitu Shrine

7. The black and white necklaces are the symbols of the power of prophecy to foresee the various occasions which are to come in the future.

Figure 12: The necklaces symbolize the power of prophecy at Nyumbanitu worship shrine. The author watches the black and white necklaces at the altar

Therefore, as a Christian worship altar is, Nyumbanitu traditional worship altar is a symbol of divine presence whereby prayers are done, and sacrifices offered to God through the ancestors. Nyumbanitu altar is decorated by all the above listed symbols to indicate its sanctity.

The symbolism of color is also vivid at Nyumbanitu worship shrine. The black cloth, the black animals used for sacrifices, and the black rob are some of the major symbols at the shrine. At Nyumbanitu traditional worship shrine, black color symbolizes the power of the ancestors to have control over living people and their affairs. When people go against their ancestors, darkness surrounds them in terms of problems they encounter in their daily lives. The solution is to appease these ancestors through the provision of

Elements of African Traditional Religion

prayers and supplications to God accompanied by sacrifices. Therefore, this indicates that color symbolism is important among the Bena and the surrounding ethnic groups that worship at Nyumbanitu worship shrine.[2]

NYUMBANITU WORSHIP IN RELATION TO OTHER WORLD RELIGIONS

What implication can we draw from the worship service done by the Bena at Nyumbanitu worship shrine in relation to the worships of other world religions and denominations of African Traditional Religion? Our observation of the altar and the words of the priests indicate that there is a great analogy between what goes on at Nyumbanitu shrine and what goes on in other world religions. First, all prayers and supplications at Nyumbanitu worship are done by human beings in relation to the Supreme Being despite the minor discrepancy of approaches which the Nyumbanitu shrine has in relation to other religions. Hence, the presence of priests who mediate people's worship of their Supreme Being is one characteristic of most denominations of African Traditional Religion.

Second, the Nyumbanitu worship altar is decorated by symbolic things that make the worship meaningful: the hoe, the spear, the small winnowing mat, the three-legged chairs, the black and white necklaces, the finger millet flour, and the black clothes. Symbols of altars vary from religion

2. Apart from the black color, Theo Sundermeier describes more colors that are used by African Traditional religious people as their symbols: the white color that symbolizes the mother's milk (food), men's semen (fertility), and the power of the ancestors who are above the normal living people, and the red color that symbolizes the blood of a menstruating woman and her fertility and family links (cf. Sundermeier, *The individual and the Community*, 46).

The Bena Worship at Nyumbanitu Shrine

to religion; and such symbols are meaningful to adherents of those religions and meaningless to people of other religions. This implies that religion is religion to adherents of that religion; and symbols are meaningful to those who embrace them.

Third, worship at Nyumbanitu shrine has a special liturgy as do other world religions. However, the liturgy is intelligible to worshippers at Nyumbanitu and neither is it intelligible to other denominations of African Traditional Religion nor to other world religions. The way worshippers at Nyumbanitu commence their worship services, the way they proceed, and the way they end their worship is not necessarily similar to other denominations and religions. The way they use their liturgical symbols: the cloth, the black rob, the black chicken, cow and goat, the flour of finger millet is different from the way other denominations and religions use their liturgical symbols. This also implies that the liturgy is a symbolic way of relating to the Supreme Being; and it is specific for every denomination and religion.

Fourth, worship at Nyumbanitu focuses its attention towards Shalula, the Creator of all that exists, as most other world religions focus their worship at God the creator of all that exists. However, Shalula (Nguluvi) is not known and is unapproachable. Shalula is approached through the hierarchy of ancestors and spirit beings that the priest mentions while at every worship. This means that the activity of Shalula upon people's lives is manifested through their interaction with the various spirit beings that perform an intermediary role.

Fifth, the holiness of Nguluvi, the God of the Bena, is manifested through the way the priests at the Nyumbanitu shrine address this God. The priests and worshippers hardly mention the name 'Nguluvi or Mulungu' in their worship service. As the Jewish religion hardly mentions the name

Elements of African Traditional Religion

'Yahweh' but mentions 'Adonai' instead, the Bena and their worship at Nyumbanitu uses the name Shalula instead of the most holy name 'Nguluvi or Mulungu.' Therefore, according to the Bena the name 'Nguluvi or Mulungu' is too holy to be mentioned.

Sixth, some of the worship practices at Nyumbanitu shrine resemble those of other world religions. For example, the taking off of shoes before entering the holy altar resembles what Moses was told by God to take off his shoes while approaching a holy place as narrated by the Bible. It also resembles what Muslims do before entering the mosque. The holy of holies room at the Nyumbanitu cave resembles the Jewish Temple that was divided into two parts: the holy place that was entered by everybody and the holy of holies that was entered by the priest once per year. Moreover, the priest entered the holy of holies in the Jewish Temple in order to pray for people's sins; in the holy of holies at Nyumbanitu cave, the priest enters only if there is a need to pray for a special problem that a person or people have encountered, and by the permission from the ancestors.

Seventh, another aspect of similarity of worship at Nyumbanitu shrine with that of other world religions is the need for purity in order to approach the shrine. The menstruating women are not allowed to enter the shrine; the shoes, veils and hats are not allowed to enter the shrine; and no any kind of alcohol is allowed to enter the altar. People with bad omen are not allowed to enter the shrine. People that approach the ancestors at the shrine have to be sober, with clear mind and good omen. Hence, all these resemble the rites stipulated in most traditions of the Jewish and Islamic religions.

Eighth, the hierarchy of spiritual beings found at Nyumbanitu worship (and in the whole African Traditional Religion) is not only limited to this worship; it is also found

The Bena Worship at Nyumbanitu Shrine

in other world religions. In Christianity, for example, Jesus, angels, the elders, and the living beings mentioned in the book of Revelation are some of the hierarchical beings that work on behalf of God. As prayers are done to God through Jesus Christ, one of the beings in the hierarchy, so are the prayers done to God through ancestors in the worship at Nyumbanitu shrine and other shrines of African Traditional Religion. This means that there are great deals of aspects that are common to all world religions despite the few peculiar features that distinguish each religion.

CONCLUSION

This chapter played an illustrative role. It illustrated the real situation of African Traditional Religion as practiced by one of the shrines in Njombe Tanzania—the Nyumbanitu worship shrine. It has been vivid in this chapter that religion and worship are specific to adherents of respective denominations and religions. Worship at Nyumbanitu has been specific for the Bena and all other ethnic groups having their origin from Nyumbanitu ancestors.

The chapter has described the two important parts of the Nyumbanitu shrine: the Nyumbanitu forest and the Nyumbanitu cave and the relationship between the two. Moreover, this chapter has made clear that the God of the Bena (Nguluvi) is too holy to be approached ad mentioned. The priests approach this God through the hierarchy of intermediaries that are mentioned in every prayer of the worship service.

The chapter has also described the symbolic representations which is the core of Nyumbanitu worship and of African Traditional Religion as a whole. The decorations of the altar with symbols and the liturgy used for worship at the shrine are characteristic of Nyumbanitu worship as a

Elements of African Traditional Religion

denomination of African Traditional religion. In this case, it can be concluded that religion is a religion to adherents of that religion; the symbols they use to represent the mysteries of their religion are meaningful to those adherents, and not necessarily meaningful to people of other religions.

REVIEW QUESTIONS

1. What is the meaning of the Term 'Nyumbanitu' (Black House) according to the descriptions of this chapter?
2. Using the various symbols used in worship at the Nyumbanitu shrine, compare symbolism in African Traditional Religion and in other World Religions, especially Abrahamic religions—Christianity, Islam, and Judaism.
3. In African Traditional Religion, "what is real is not visible and what is visible is just appearance." How is this statement plausible in what goes on at Nyumbanitu worship shrine?
4. Discuss the brief historical background of the way worship was officially recognized among the Bena under Kiswaga ancestral clans.
5. At Nyumbanitu worship shrine, Shalula is the creator of all that exists, is unknowable and is unapproachable. Discuss this statement in relation to the various attributes of God in African Traditional Religion.

5

African Cosmology

INTRODUCTION

IN THE PREVIOUS TWO chapters, the focus was on the concept of God in Africa and the ways through which Africans worship this God at Nyumbanitu shrine. Through the two chapters above, we concluded that missionaries did not bring God to Africa because God was there before they arrived; rather, God brought them to Africa for a special purpose: to proclaim Christianity and the legacy of Jesus Christ. In this chapter we will look in a more detail on African cosmology. We will define the term cosmology, discuss the concept of creation as viewed by Africans, and analyze the relationship between God and the hierarchy of spiritual beings: God, divinities, spirits, ancestors and their relationship with the living people. The discussion on these aspects of the African cosmology will enable us to move towards looking at the concepts of Revelation and Salvation as understood by Africans.

Elements of African Traditional Religion

WHAT IS THE MEANING OF COSMOLOGY?

When we want to know about the term 'cosmology' we need to know the components of this term. The word 'cosmology' is derived from two Greek words 'cosmos' that means 'world' and 'logos' means "study". In this background, the word "cosmology" means the study of the world and its components. In other words, it is the study of the worldview of the people. How do they view the world and its components? How does this view affect their general life and practice?

Wilbur O'Donovan clearly defines a worldview thus: A world view "is the way he (or she) understands and interprets things which happen to him (or her) and to other people. It is a person's belief about what is real and what is not real."[1] Considering O'Donovan's definition above we can note that people are different in this world, they live in different locations, and brought up in different contexts. This means that no one person can know the whole world. People can know and be oriented to particular locations and particular situations. These are what make the worldview of those people.

When we talk of African worldview, we mean the way Africans understand various aspects surrounding them. It means the way they look at eh relationship they have with God and the hierarchy of spirits ancestors and the living, the way they look at creation, etc. In this understanding of the African worldview, we discern the real African and his or her personality as opposed to people of other contexts.

AFRICAN VIEW OF CREATION

Africans believe that the earth did not happen in its own as a matter of chance. They believe that it was created by

1. O'Donovan, *Biblical Christianity*, iii.

African Cosmology

God. To them, to speak of the universe being created by God is to speak about the creator. Over the whole Africa, creation is one of the most acknowledged works of God. Africans acknowledge strongly that the cosmos was created by God. They do this through mentioning God as Creator and through mentioning God in prayers. The metaphor of the potter describes God's creative activity.

Another aspect is the way people see this God as potter and how they demonstrate this capability of God. Banyarwanda women (of Rwanda) normally put water in some containers before they go to bed so that God may use that water in order to create children for them. This water is known as the "water of God." In these events, God is known as the provider of Children. People believe that there was nothing at all before God created the world. This means that the concept of creation ex-nihilo was there, especially among the Nuer of Sudan, the Shona of Zimbabwe, and Banyarwanda of Rwanda. These ethnic groups believe that God did not only create the material universe, but the established laws of nature and human customs. The Ashanti of Ghana believe that God created all things in an orderly fashion; no error in creation according to these people. The Zulu people also believe that the institution of marriage and circumcision were done by God. Moreover, they believe that God continues to create and appreciate the ongoing creation of God. In this case, the above descriptions indicate that God as viewed by Africans is the sole originator of all what exists.

AFRICAN VIEW OF GOD AND THE SUN

Sunshine is one of the expressions of God's providence in Africa. The sun appears everyday providing light, warmth, change of seasons, and growth of crops. The understanding of most African ethnic groups is that the sun is the one that moves not the earth. The Akan of Ghana call God "the shining one" to signify that God is the one that provides light. For them, the shining of the sun symbolizes the presence and providence of God. In a similar way, the Ankole, the Haya and Nyambo call God "Kazoba" that means sun. In this case, the sun is the major symbol for God (to God's power or strength). Africans use a metaphoric and symbolic representation of God through the use of the sun. In this way, the sun is not regarded as God, in any way, but as a symbol of God. Most Africans are used to praying every early morning, afternoon, and evening and even during doing certain events. Most of these prayers are directed to God symbolically through the sun. This means that God is more powerful and controls the sun. God is invisible and the sun is visible. The African Traditional Religious philosophy is clearly articulated in the way people view at the sun and symbolically use it to represent God. What is real is invisible and what is visible is just appearance!

The above discussion indicates that there is a very close relationship between the sun and God, and the sun and people. A proper understanding of the relationship between the three aspects is a key to the understanding of the indigenous concept of God. However, unfortunately some scholars, missionaries, etc. have misunderstood this concept and have thought that Africans are "worshiper of the sun." Some of these misunderstanding appear in their literature.

The name "*Kazoba*" which is noble name for God among the Haya, Ankole, Zinza and Subi is known by some scholars as the name for a spirit. Another similar claim by such scholars is that those people who regard the sun as symbol for God do not know the way to differentiate between the sun and God. But this claim is strongly denied on the ground that the whole practice and language used portray

African Cosmology

the difference between God and sun. In such cases, *Kazoba* is the name for God while *Izoba* is the name for the sun.

Following the above differentiation one can see that the statements from some scholars that Africans worship the sun and pray to it are unjust and unrealistic. The differentiation between the sun and God is obvious, that they cannot be worshippers of the sun, nor their religion be described as "sun worship" religion. In this perspective, some African people know that the sun in an inaccessible source of light perfectly and an adequate symbol of the transcendence of God which the sun signifies and whose transcendence is experienced through looking at the sun. Hence opposite to the sun worshippers, Africans used the sun as a symbol (means) to worship God, but clearly knowing the power and majesty of God behind the sun.

GOD, DIVINITIES, SPIRITS, ANCESTORS AND THE LIVING PEOPLE IN AFRICAN COSMOLOGY

The above-mentioned beings indicate the hierarchical structure or order through which God deals with humanity according to African cosmology.[2] We will discuss each hierarchy and the way it relates to God and with humanity according to African worldview.

Divinities

Most people wonder as to where we should put a line of demarcation between divinities and spirits. But more briefly, the nature and role of divinities in relation to God and human beings is distinct. The divinity is a locally oriented

2. Cf. Sundermeier, *The Individual and the Community*, 104–5.

being and is a means to an end. God is an end. The divinity therefore has a local name which appears to limit its scope to the locality. Divinities are ministers, each in its own sphere or department and are heads of departments.

Each divinity has an independent role to play without contradicting to other divinities. There are also intermediaries between God and man especially in reference to their particular function (department). The correct interpretation of divinities is that they hold a half-way house which is not to be a permanent resting house for human soul. Human soul rests but just a half-way rest house, man needs to go further to God. Technically, divinities are only a means to an end and not end in themselves. When a divinity is made an end then misconception is done. In this case, the function and role of divinities is related to biblical spiritual beings (angels) who are also not end in themselves but means to an end (God).

Some scholars call biblical spiritual beings as "sub-divinities" and that the name "divinity" is only preferable for God who has a pure divinity. Moreover, scholars claim that these divinities conceived by African Traditional Religious function in a similar way with those of heavenly Christian and Jewish cosmologies. Thus, African mythologies are full of divinities. To Africans, a divinity is a reality in nature and in history. Divinities were created and have no independent power of their own. They depend on God for their power.

Some departments or functions for divinities include the following:

(i) Agriculture—the divinity for agriculture concerns itself with the welfare of crops

(ii) Animals—the divinity that is concerned with animals

（iii） The divinity for lake and rivers—this is concerned with the welfare of the lake and rivers

(iv) Disaster and forest

In a more general sense, we can say that in order for us now to understand the way divinities in African cosmology work, we need to understand the way biblical spiritual beings work and interact with God and with other beings, including human beings. This is because there is a great similarity in their functions.

Spirits

Spirits is the second group of beings in the hierarchy after divinities. There are two kinds of spirits depending on their origin: Those who were born as human beings (ghosts), and those who were created by God. African Tradition Religious cosmology conceives that spirits of human kind form the majority part as compared to spirits created by God.

Many spirits manifest themselves through human mediums. There are malevolent and benevolent spirits. And it is said that if properly treated they can withdraw illnesses from humanity. Some spirits have the power to predict future events and have no limit of knowledge as human beings are. This means that spirits are beyond physical limitations, but they can be approached through human mediums.

The above characteristics of spirits have led some scholars to claim that Africans worship spirits. In its real sense, spirits are not God and are neither worshipped. These are mere spirits which have received special assignments and are controlled by God.

Elements of African Traditional Religion

Ancestors

A belief in an ongoing relationship between the ancestors living in an invisible world and people living in the visible world is a living reality among Africans. Ancestors are part of the respective society. However, several questions have been asked regarding ancestors as components of the hierarchy. One of such question includes the following: Are the African people worship these ancestors or venerate them? Some scholars say that an ancestor is the one that joins the community of the "living dead" in the invisible world. Ancestors are those who are remembered by their societies and families. They belong to the invisible world and are close to the spirits (but are not spirits).

John Mbiti also writes thus about ancestors: "a person who is physically dead but alive in the memory of those who knew him or her in life as well as being alive in the world of the spirits. So long as the living dead is thus remembered, he or she is in the state of personal immortality."[3]

Ancestors matter most in the *family level*. Ancestors are part and parcel of the living people and live closer to the spirits. Ancestors want people to honour God and spirits in order to live a good moral life. Ancestral spirits have always been known to be the cause of many calamities affecting the clans. Misfortunes and diseases are not seen as to be coming for their own sake, but as means to inform the living that something is wrong in their relationship with the living dead. In such cases the diviners have an important role in identifying the cause as well as the means to make the necessary reconciliation. The roles of the diviners are closely related to the medicine men and women who help in giving treatment to those afflicted with diseases, misfortunes and sorcery or witches.

3. Mbiti, *African Traditional Religion*, 25.

African Cosmology

Joseph Healey and Donard Sybertz elaborate the interaction between these ancestral spirits and the living people as follows:

> The intervention of the ancestors is invoked at the time of birth of a child, when there is sickness, when starting a journey, when making a fortune, at planting season, at the harvesting, marriage, death, etc. The ancestors are seen as part of the family and living with the community and being to influence one's life for good or will. The ancestors provide counsel and help grant prosperity and order to those who observe their laws and traditions. But they can injure them if ignored or insulted. If human beings disobey them, the ancestors can punish them by reducing the general well-being; it is very important for Africans to have good relations with their ancestors. Thus, the necessity of ancestor veneration.[4]

The conclusion of the above quotation responds to the prior asked question whether ancestors are worshiped or venerated. Hence, ancestors are not God and are not worthy the worship, but only veneration and remembrance.[5]

Through mediums, prayers, dreams, and even names Africans communicate with the ancestors believing that they are always watching them. This is mostly because ancestors act as God's agents and take part in keeping and controlling the universe. This truth about the African Traditional Religion is also attested by Healey and Sybertz when they write thus: "In traditional African society remembrance and respect for the living dead are intimately connected with ancestor veneration. Everything in life is

---

4. Healey & Sybertz, *Towards an African Narrative Theology*, 214–215.

5. Sundermeier, *The Individual and the Community*, 120–136.

Elements of African Traditional Religion

linked to the ancestors, who do not take the place of the 'Supreme God,' but are mediators (. . .). Human beings must have solidarity with their ancestors."[6]

Ancestors, though live together with other family members, are not in the physical world; they are in the spiritual world. Since they are not in the ordinary world, therefore, the way of approaching them must be different. They are spirits and have to be approached as spirits and not as normal human beings. Some people wrongly think that the cult of ancestors is the central core of African Traditional Religion. However, the truth is that the cult of ancestors does not make a central core of African Traditional Religion; and it is a great error to identify ancestral cult as a religion and as a central core of African Traditional Religion.

The proper meaning of ancestors can be best derived from the Africans' belief that life does not always end up with the human's physical death; but life is also beyond death. This means that death never finishes an African person's life. Through the ancestral cult, it is shown that life extends beyond death and communication with ancestors confirms the extension of life's communion and communication.

The important question as we close the section for ancestors is this: Has the concept of ancestors found a proper place in the Christian teachings, or mere misunderstandings? In other words: Is there any place for Jesus maintaining the relationship with the living and the dead? In fact one can note that African Traditional Religion's doctrine of Ancestors has not found a proper place in the life of African Christians because the missionaries tended to confuse and generalize ancestors and spirits, considering all of them as Satanic. They endeavored to cut off the relationship and communion with ancestors. What we need to emphasize here is that it is very difficult to separate an African with

6. Ibid., 214.

African Cosmology

his/her worldview. If the church does not recognize the cult of ancestors, people will be forced to practice it in secret. Hence, this secret practice will be the cause for continuity of African Traditional Religion in Christianity.

CONCLUSION

This chapter has indicated that the belief in the Supreme Being is also a belief in the hierarchy of divine beings. Human beings interact with the this God through these divine beings. Most of the ritual or symbolic actions done in the lives of the Africans are directed to these divine beings. Through their interaction with ancestors, divinities, the living dead and spirits, Africans interact with Supreme Being. This is mainly because the life force of the Supreme Being is bestowed upon all living beings including the divine beings in the hierarchy.

The chapter has also emphasized that despite the slight disparity of traditional values and culture among African peoples yet they all worship only one God. This means that the difference that is visible is just appearance, what is real is the same to all African cultures and is invisible. African peoples have a difference in the appearance of their ritual practices and worship of the Supreme Being, but they have the same essence of their idea and reality of what they practice.

REVIEW QUESTIONS

1. What does it mean by the word 'cosmology?'
2. Discuss the way in which in which creation is viewed by African Traditional Religion.
3. Discuss the hierarchy of beings in God's dealing with humanity according to African Traditional Religion.

6

Concepts of Revelation and Salvation

INTRODUCTION

THE CONCEPTS OF REVELATION and salvation are important in any religion. A religion must be able to explain the way in which the Supreme object of worship makes itself known to the adherents of that religion. It also must be able to explain the way people are delivered from various calamities around them. This means that there must be something of the Divine revealed upon people who embrace that religion.[1] Therefore a better description of these concepts provides a better misunderstanding of these religions.

In this chapter we will discuss briefly the two above-mentioned concepts as related to the African worldview. We will start wit the concept of revelation and then that of salvation.

---

1. Magesa, *African Religion*, 24–27.

Concepts of Revelation and Salvation

THE CONCEPT OF REVELATION

To reveal oneself, according to the meaning of the word, it is so to make oneself known or open to the view of people from the state of being unknown and hidden. In religious point of view it mostly refers to the Supreme Being and the way it manifests its presence in the midst of created beings. Revelation has special room in African Traditional Religion. Africans believe that the revelation of God came in the past and still comes to them in various ways, e.g., in dreams, visions, nature, prophecy, and symbols and myths.

However, we can ask, is there at all any revelation in African Traditional Religion? Does the Supreme Being of the Africans reveal to Africans so that they can glance the presence and providence? The view of most Christian theologians is that there is no salvation outside the church. Such theologians use Christian scriptures to justify that in other religions God has not revealed oneself and people in those religions live in darkness. They have not known God the Creator of Heavens and earth.

In fact, the old view from the missionaries who first approached Africans with their own pre-conceived notions and saw that African Traditional Religion as a religion without God is one of the great distortions of God's revelation. However, some Christian theologians like Paul Tillich and Panenberg see that there is a possibility for revelation outside the Church. Their main base is on Natural Revelation. According to these Christian scholars, God's revelation is unlimited. It is universal. On this base, these theologians claim that an individual can obtain revelation through the movements of history. These movements become windows though which the words and teachings of God come to us, albeit as a glimpse if not full. This means that even Plato, a philosopher whom Augustine spoke of him as being a

Christian before Christianity and Isaiah, were instruments of God to the disclosure of God. Isaiah predicted that God will come to us through God's servant.

In cementing the presence of revelation in African Traditional Religion some African theologians find Christ in African Traditional Religion, but a hidden Christ. According to these theologians, if Christ is the manifestation of God in Christian understanding, and God revealed to Africans through natural revelation embedded in their culture, then Christ implicitly revealed to Africans. To Africans, Jesus Christ is present but hidden; Jesus Christ is *Deus Absconditus* (hidden God). This indicates that the conception of Jesus as God according to the Christian teachings makes it difficult to speak about revelation in African Traditional Religion without considering about Jesus Christ.[2]

Revelation in African Traditional Religion has been experienced through dreams and visions. A good example of revelation in African Traditional Religion is Chief Kimweri of Tanga in Tanzania who dreamt about the coming of missionaries and Christianity in Usambara area. The vision led him to prophesying about the kind of people that would come and the aim of their coming. This also indicates that in African Traditional religion both revelation and prophecies are encountered.

However, all the assertions above are good indicators that Africans believe that revelation is possible, but only through God's initiatives to all people in the world. It is God's plan and involvement in the history of people in various stages. This also indicates that God's involvement with the Jews and the Christians does not limit God's involvement with other people because God is not only God for the Jews and Christians. God is God for the whole world's creation, and God's revelation is both limitless and

2. Cf. Bahemuka, "The Hidden Christ," (1998).

Concepts of Revelation and Salvation

incomprehensible. The God of the Jews and Christians is the same God as the one whom the African ancestors worshipped and served in their indigenous religion. Logically conceived, God could not have created these African people and left them without any glimpse of revelation to them. This implies that God revealed to them through their own religion. Surely, God did not leave them in ignorance!

THE CONCEPT OF SALVATION

Michael Foucault quoted in Mary Esperandio in her article "Spiritual Care of the Self: A New Form of Religious Experience in Globalized Post-Modernity?" asserts thus in regard to religion and salvation: "Being a religion of salvation, [religion] (. . .) should lead the person from one reality to another, from life to death, from time to eternity. In order to achieve this [religion] imposes several conditions and rules of conduct with the goal of obtaining a certain transformation of Self."[3] This means that the adherents of religion are not to accept and believe the truths embraced, but also demonstrate commitment to such beliefs and truths embraced.

The concept of salvation is central to every religion and to all believers of that religion. To some tribes, e.g., the ones from the northern part of Tanzania–the Bahaya, Banyambo, Banyankole, Baziza, etc., the concept of salvation is known to them through experience. This experience is more vivid in their daily lives. Some words used for this purpose by the above-mentioned tribes include: *Obulokozi* (noun-salvation) and Okulokola (verb-to be saved from deadly thing or event). These words were used

---

3. Esperandio, "Spiritual Care of the Self," 52.

by these tribes before the coming of Christianity in these communities.

When Christianity came, the missionaries used the same words. Humanly and practically speaking, salvation to the above named tribes meant a state of escaping away from deadly things. Among the Sukuma and Nyamwezi of Tabora Shinyanga and Mwanza in Tanzania there are stories about the Zimwi Ngara, a deadly animal. These stories explain the way the concept of salvation can be clearly perceived. Salvation from or escape from the encounter with the Zimwi Ngara is salvation.

Moreover, as an escape from dangerous calamities, the concept refers to various aspects that face African lives including the following:

> inconsistencies of the weather, natural disasters such as droughts and floods, hazards caused by encounters with wild beasts, hunger and poverty which result in a high infant mortality rate (Africans have a great desire for children, especially sons), lack of employment, bad luck or failure in life's ventures, unforeseen conditions which give rise to practical problems, other types of evils and misfortunes, conditions which experience has taught them to find oppressive and from which they seek relief or salvation.[4]

Mgeyekwa's statement above indicates that salvation as conceived by African Traditional Religion depends on that what endeavors to disturb the existing harmony. The mentioned aspects disturb harmony in the fabric of relationship in African societies. Hence, salvation mostly means a means to escape from the effects of such calamities.

Apart from salvation as being an escape from deadly things, salvation can also be conceived as being an

---

4. Mgeyekwa, "The Understanding of Salvation," 122.

Concepts of Revelation and Salvation

acceptance. For African Traditional Religious believers, salvation "implies acceptance in the community of the living and the living dead, deliverance from the power of the evil spirits, and a possession of a life force."[5] In this case, because of the fear of being threatened, believers of African Traditional Religion are indebted to offering sacrifices to God through offering them to spirits and the living-dead in order to avoid misfortunes in their lives.

It must be clearly understood that wearing charms and amulets or hanging them on the lintels of their houses are common phenomena in order to be delivered from evil forces. "One is first accepted to the community of the living," writes Adeyemo, "by being good to one's neighbor, and secondly accepted among the community of the dead ancestors by remembering them through libations, prayers, and offerings."[6] Therefore, the fear of deadly things, the fear of witches, the fear of misfortunes inflicted by ancestors upon people in a particular tribe or family, make the concept of salvation one of the important aspects of consideration.

CONCLUSION

The concepts of revelation and salvation are not the same in all religions. Every religion has its own concepts. There are such concepts in Judaism, in Christianity, and in all other world religions. This chapter endeavored do demonstrate the way African traditional religion conceives of such concepts. The concept of revelation in African Traditional Religion is mainly based on the way the Supreme Being makes oneself known to the adherents of that religion. God revealed oneself in the past through the creation of all what

---

5. Adeyemo, *Salvation in African Tradition*, 94.
6. Ibid., 93.

Elements of African Traditional Religion

exists now. However, this revelation did not end in the past. It is a continuous process.

The revelation of God to humanity still continues through various ways: dreams, visions, existing nature, prophecy, symbols, and symbolic actions done by religious adherents (rituals). This means that though the Supreme Being of African Traditional Religion is far remote from the created beings, yet this Supreme Being is quite imminent through manifold ways contrary to the false conceptions of the early missionaries.

Salvation in African Traditional Religion is understood in terms of God's deliverance of people from life-threatening calamities. It is the maintenance of harmony in the interaction of community members and their interaction with the divine beings. The practice of rituals to appease the angry beings in order not to inflict punishments upon them is another way of seeking deliverance. Therefore, the understanding of both salvation and revelation in the African traditional Religion depends on the world view of adherents of this religion and can hardly be clear to those outsiders.

REVIEW QUESTIONS

1. God has revealed oneself through African Traditional Religion. Discuss this statement in relation to the Christian Doctrine of *exra Ecclessium nulla sallus* (outside the Church there is no salvation).

2. Differentiate between Natural and Special revelations of God. What kind of relvelation is found in African Traditional Religion?

3. Did Jesus Christ reveal himself to Africans before the coming of Christianity in the African soil? Discuss

Concepts of Revelation and Salvation

this question in relation to the views of theological scholars on the concepts of *Deus absconditus* and *Deus revelatus*.

4. Why do you think the concept of salvation is central to every religion? Discuss this question with special reference to African Traditional Religion.

5. With concrete examples discuss the way in which the concept of salvation is understood according to African Traditional Religion.

6. Compare the understanding of salvation in African Traditional Religion and other World Religions, especially Abrahamic Religions (Judaism, Islam, and Christianity).

7

Conclusion

IN THIS BOOK WE have attempted a discussion about African Traditional Religion and its major practices. The major aim of the book was to clarify what Africans traditionally believe and what do they practice. We have argued in this book that the old view that sees African Traditional Religion as being a religion without a clear concept of God and proper system of worship is being superficial and with a lack of understanding of what other people believe and practice. In this case we stressed that the African philosophy is clear about their faith and practice; what is visible is not real and that what is visible is just appearance. Reality is beyond the visible realm of humanity.

The discussion about rituals, symbols and myths have demonstrated that religion is unique in the way through which people approach the reality around them. By the description of worship and symbolism at Nyumbanitu shrine the book has shown that African religious symbolism describes the uniqueness of communication and relationship between God, divinities, spirits, ancestors and living

Conclusion

people. It is this interaction between these hierarchies that characterizes the cosmology of African people.

The major question that intrigues us is this: Why do people jeopardize other people's religions? It has been vivid in the discussion within this book that ignorance of what is inside that religion is the major cause of this jeopardizing habit. Missionaries came to Africa with their pre-conceived notions from their own countries. Through their pre-conceived notions, they found African culture and religion hardly does justice to what really goes on in that culture and religion.

The book has also made clear that God as Supreme Being of the Africans has a lot of attributes that qualify African traditional religion as the worship of the true God worshiped by other major world religions. The names such as Nguluvi, Mulungu, Kazoba, etc., are names of God that emanates from the experiences of God's providence in the respective tribes. At Nyumbanitu the one Supreme Being is worshipped by the Bena and their nearby tribes performing all the required symbolic actions regarding the actual worship in its real sense. In this case the same God worshipped by Africans has various names and is worshipped in various traditional ways depending on the experiences of people.

As we conclude this book, it is better to emphasize that African culture and religion need to be respected if one is to preserve the dignity of the African humanity. African culture needs to be respected because it is the foundation of any subsequent religion that enters the African continent. This accounts for the difficulty of people to abandon African traditional practices when they decide to embrace a foreign religion such as Christianity. Building a concrete Christianity in an African context depends solely on the way those doing mission work properly, analyze, and build their teachings on the foundation of African people's world view in a way that provides adequate answers to their current concerns. Therefore, it is through building on African people's world faith and practice that Christianity will free itself from producing half-Christians or Christians that undergo a double life.

Bibliography

Adeyemo, Tukunboh. *Salvation in African Tradition*. Nairobi: Evangel Publishing House, 1979.

All Africa Conference of Churches, *Problems and Promises of Africa: Towards and Beyond the Year 2000*. Nairobi: All Africa Conference of Churches, 1993.

Bahemuka, Judith M. "The Hidden Christ in African Traditional Religion," 2–16. In *Jesus in African Christianity: Experimentation and Diversity in African Christology*, edited by J.N.K. Mugambi and Laurent Magesa. Nairobi: Action Publishers, 1998.

Bahemuka, Judith Mbula, *Our Religious Heritage*. Lagos: Thomas and Nelson, 1982.

Brown, David, *A Guide to Religions*. London: SPCK, 1975.

Chepkwony, Adam K. Arap, "African Religion, the Root Paradigm for Inculturation Theology: Prospects for the 21st Century," 30–53. In *Challenges and Prospects of the Church in Africa: Theological Reflections of the 21st Century*, edited by Nahashon W. Ndung'u and Philomena N.Mwaura. Nairobi: Paulines Publications Africa, 2005.

Chepkwony, Adam K. Arap, "Forgiveness: The Divine Gift of Peace, Reconciliation, and Healing," 131–147. In *Religion, Conflict, and Democracy in Modern Africa: The Role of Civil Society in Political Engagement*, edited by Samuel K. Elolia. Eugene, Oregon: Pickwick, 2012.

Cragg, Kenneth, *The Christian and Other Religion: The Measure of Christ*. London & Oxford: A.R. Mowbray & Co.Ltd, 1977.

Esperandio, Mary, "Spiritual Care of the Self: A New Form of Religious Experience in Globalized Post-Modernity?" 47–55. *In Religion in a Globalized World: Transfers & Transformations Integration & Resistence*. Oslo: Novus Press, 2008.

Frostin, Per, *Teologi som Befriar: Efterlamnade Texter*. Religio 41, Skrifter utgivna av Teologiska Institutionen i Lund, 1994.

Bibliography

Fue, Peter, "The Sermon on the Mount—an African Perspective," 129–140. In Eero Junkkaala, *Introduction to the New Testament-with African Perspectives*. Iringa: Iringa University College, 2011.

Furre, Berge, "The Brazilian 'Universal Church of the Kingdom of God': From Suburb in Rio de Janeiro to the entire Globe," 37–45. In *Religion in a Globalized Age: Transfers & Transformations Integration & Resistance*. Oslo: Novus Press, 2008.

Gehman, Richard J. *African Traditional Religion in Biblical Perspectives*. Kijabe,Kenya: Kesho Publications, 1986.

Gichure, Peter I. "Religion and Politics in Africa: The Rise of Ethno-Religions," 34–47. In *Religion and Politics in Africa: Theological Reflections for the 21st Century*, edited by Peter I. Gichure & Diane B. Stinton. Nairobi: Paulines Publications Africa, 2008.

Grebe, Karl and Wilfred Fon, African Traditional Religion and Christian Counseling," 93–146. In *Insights in African Ethnography: Occasional Papers from Ethno-Info No.2*, edited by Barbara Moore, 1997.

Healey Joseph and Donard Syybertz, *Towards and African Narrative Theology*. Nairobi: Paulines Publications Africa, 1996.

Holm, Jean, "Preface," vi–viii. In *Women in Religion*, edited by Jean Holm with John Bowker. London: Continuum, 1994.

Idowu Bolaji E. *African Traditional Religion: A Definition*. Maryknoll, New York: Orbis Books, 1973.

Katoke, I.K. "The Coming of the Gospel and African Reaction," 97–118. In *Essays on Church and Society in Tanzania*, edited by C.K. Omari. Arusha: Evangelical Lutheran Church in Tanzania, 1976.

Khamalwa, Wotsuna, "Religion, Traditional Healers, and the AIDS Pandemic in Uganda," 82–95. In *Religion and Health in Africa: Reflections for Theology in the 21st Century*, edited by Adam arp Chepkwony. Nairobi: Paulines Publications Africa, 2006.

King, Noel, *African Cosmos: An Introduction to Religion in Africa*. Belmont: California: Wadsworth , 1986.

Kolie, Cece, "Jesus as Healer," 128–150. *Faces of Jesus in Africa*. Faith and Culture Series, edited by Robert Schreiter. Maryknoll, New York: Orbis Books, 1991.

Kunin, Seth D. "Anthropological and Sociological Theories of Religion," 55– 93. In *A Companion to Religious Studies and Theology*, edited by Helen K. Bond, Seth D. Kunin, and Francesca Aran Murphy. Edinburgh: Edinburgh University Press, 2003.

Kyomo, Andrew A. "Oral Tradition in the Old Testament and in the African Religion," 75–86. In Eero Junkkaala, *Introduction* to the Old Testament—with African Perspectives. Iringa: Iringa University College, 2010.

Lama, Amen Anza. "The Impact of Christianity on African Traditional Education," 65– 86. In *Essays on Church and Society in Tanzania*, edited by C.K. Omari. Arusha: Evangelical Lutheran Church in Tanzania, 1976.

Magesa, Laurenti, *African Religion: The Moral Traditions of Abundant Life*. Nairobi: Paulines Publications, 1997.

Makumba, Maurice M., *Introduction to African Philosophy*. Nairobi: Paulines Publications Africa, 2007.

Mbiti John, *African Religions and Philosophy*. Nairobi: Heinemann, 1969.

Mbiti, John, *Concepts of God in Africa*. London: SPCK, 1970.

Mbiti, John S. *Introduction to African Religion*. Nairobi: Heinemann, 1975.

Mbiti, John, *Introduction to African Religion*. Second Edition. Nairobi: East African Educational Publishers, 1991.

Mbwilo. *Funzo la Kiswahili kwa Methali, Nahau na Vitendawili*. Dar es Salaam: Mbwilo Publishers, 2011.

Mgeyekwa, Gabriel E. "The Understanding of Salvation in African traditional Religions," 121–128. In Eero Junkkaala, *Introduction to the New Testament—with African Perspectives*. Iringa: Iringa University College, 2011.

Mligo, Elia Shabani, *Jesus and the Stigmatized: Reading the Gospel of John in a Context of HIV/AIDS-Related Stigmatization in Tanzania*. Eugene, Oregon: Pickwick Publications, 2011.

Mligo, Elia Shabani, *The Pride of African Traditional Medicine: Exploring the Role of African Traditional Medicine Men and Women in God's Healing Ministry within the African Context*. Saarbrucken, Germany: LAP Lambert Academic Publishing, 2013.

Mojola, Aloo, "The Global Context and Its Consequences for Old Testament Translation," 57–82. In *Global Hermeneutics? Reflections and Consequences*, edited by Knut Holter and Louis C. Jonker. Atlanta, Georgia: Society of Biblical Literature, 2010.

Mwaura, Philomena N. "Ritual Healing and Redefinition of Individual Personality in African Instituted Churches in Kenya," 64–81. In *Religion and Health in Africa: Reflections for Theology in the 21st Century*, edited by Adam arap Chepkwony. Nairobi: Paulines Publications Africa, 2006.

Mugambi, J.N.K. *Christianity and African Culture*. Nairobi: Action, 2002.

Bibliography

Mugambi, J.N.K and N. Kirima. *The African Religious Heritage*. Nairobi: Oxford, 1976.

O'Donovan, Wilbur. *Biblical Christianity in African Perspective*. Carlisle: Paternoster Press, 1996.

Sanders, E.P. *The Historical Figure of Jesus*. London: Penguin Books, 1993.

Schreiter, Robert J. *The New Catholicity: Theology between the Global and the Local*. Maryknoll, New York: Orbis Books, 2004.

Schreiter, Robert J. *Constructing Local Theologies*. Maryknoll, New York: Orbis Books, 1985.

Stinton, Diane B. "Jesus as Healer: Reflections on Religion and Health in East Africa Today," 13-35. In *Religion and Health in Africa: Reflections for Theology in the 21st Century*, edited by Adam K. arap Chepkwony. Nairobi: Paulines Publications Africa, 2006.

Sundermeier, Theo. *The Individual and the Community in African Traditional Religions*. Hamburg: LIT, 1998.

The Illustrated Book of Man in Society, edited by James Mitchell. London: Mitchell Beazley Encyclopaedias, 1982.

Walligo, John Mary. "Making the Church that is truly African," 11-30. In *Inculturation: Its Meaning and Urgency*, edited by John M. Walligo and Others. Kampla: St. Paul Publication Africa, 1986.

www.ingramcontent.com/pod-product-compliance
Lightning Source LLC
Chambersburg PA
CBHW070920160426
43193CB00011B/1537